DATE DUE

GAYLORD			PRINTED IN U.S.A.

Remembering Ritalin

. . .

A Doctor and Generation Rx
Reflect on Life and Psychiatric Drugs

. . .

Lawrence H. Diller, MD

A PERIGEE BOOK

A PERIGEE BOOK
Published by the Penguin Group
Penguin Group (USA) Inc.
375 Hudson Street, New York, New York 10014, USA

Penguin Group (Canada), 90 Eglinton Avenue East, Suite 700, Toronto, Ontario M4P 2Y3, Canada (a division of Pearson Penguin Canada Inc.) • Penguin Books Ltd., 80 Strand, London WC2R 0RL, England • Penguin Group Ireland, 25 St. Stephen's Green, Dublin 2, Ireland (a division of Penguin Books Ltd.) • Penguin Group (Australia), 250 Camberwell Road, Camberwell, Victoria 3124, Australia (a division of Pearson Australia Group Pty. Ltd.) • Penguin Books India Pvt. Ltd., 11 Community Centre, Panchsheel Park, New Delhi—110 017, India • Penguin Group (NZ), 67 Apollo Drive, Rosedale, Auckland 0632, New Zealand (a division of Pearson New Zealand Ltd.) • Penguin Books (South Africa) (Pty.) Ltd., 24 Sturdee Avenue, Rosebank, Johannesburg 2196, South Africa

Penguin Books Ltd., Registered Offices: 80 Strand, London WC2R 0RL, England

While the author has made every effort to provide accurate telephone numbers and Internet addresses at the time of publication, neither the publisher nor the author assumes any responsibility for errors or for changes that occur after publication. Further, the publisher does not have any control over and does not assume any responsibility for author or third-party websites or their content.

Copyright © 2011 by Lawrence Diller, MD
Text design by Laura K. Corless

First edition: May 2011

Library of Congress Cataloging-in-Publication Data

Diller, Lawrence H.
  Remembering Ritalin : a doctor and generation Rx reflect on life and psychiatric drugs / Lawrence H. Diller.— 1st ed.
    p. cm.
  "A Perigee book."
  Includes bibliographical references and index.
  ISBN 978-0-399-53664-9 (Perigee hardcover)
  1. Attention-deficit hyperactivity disorder—Treatment—Case studies.   2. Methylphenidate—Side effects.   I. Title.
  [DNLM: 1. Attention Deficit Disorder with Hyperactivity—drug therapy—Case Reports.
2. Methylphenidate—adverse effects—Case Reports.   3. Methylphenidate—therapeutic use—Case Reports. WS 350.8.A8]
  RJ506.H9D539   2011
  618.92'8589061—dc22   2010054224

PRINTED IN THE UNITED STATES OF AMERICA
10 9 8 7 6 5 4 3 2 1

Neither the publisher nor the author is engaged in rendering professional advice or services to the individual reader. The ideas, procedures, and suggestions contained in this book are not intended as a substitute for consulting with your physician. All matters regarding your health require medical supervision. Neither the author nor the publisher shall be liable or responsible for any loss or damage allegedly arising from any information or suggestion in this book.

Most Perigee books are available at special quantity discounts for bulk purchases for sales promotions, premiums, fund-raising, or educational use. Special books, or book excerpts, can also be created to fit specific needs. For details, write: Special Markets, Penguin Group (USA) Inc., 375 Hudson Street, New York, New York 10014.

To Beth, Vivian, and Denise

For steadfast support and caring over the years

ACKNOWLEDGMENTS

The young adults/ex-patients of mine who agreed to be interviewed (no one refused me) are responsible for this book. Therefore, I must first profusely thank Daniel W., Lauren, Jennifer, Evan, Cannon, Robby, Richard, Daniel B., Tim, and Maggie. Two mothers, Barbara and Cindy, also spoke to me at length, and I thank them, too.

Russell Barkley, PhD, was willing to talk to me at length once again (he's helped me before) for this project. His experience, wisdom, and readiness to speak on the record about social and ethical issues surrounding ADHD and Ritalin make him unique among the experts in this field.

I am grateful for the time spent and feedback from the professional and lay readers of the manuscript: Jack Obedzinski, MD; Sam Goldstein, PhD; Jennifer Poyer-Ackerman; Jill Delevaux; and Justin Hourany. Jennifer and Jill, in particular as "parent" readers, could have been copy editors in previous lives.

Sabina Morganti, MFCC; John Weil, PhD; Mary Jane Nunes-Temple, MFCC; and I have been meeting as a consultation and support group for over ten years. Their monthly insights and support have helped me maintain a balance and direction in the often choppy professional waters I've navigated during the past decade (and through three books).

I thank the sandwich makers and John DiVicenzo, the owner, of Genova Delicatessen in Walnut Creek, just down the street from my office, who have fed me lunch for over twenty-two years. The deli was also the site of several of the interviews for this book.

Sam Hawgood, ex-chief of pediatrics, now the dean of the University of California, San Francisco Medical School, has continued to support my clinical faculty appointment to UCSF for the past decade. My faculty status allowed me online access to the vast University of California library, especially the online periodicals, which made visits to the physical library unnecessary for the research in this book. I note over thirteen years since writing *Running on Ritalin* how much my research methodologies have changed as a result of the World Wide Web.

My sons, Martin and Louie, are now twenty-three and twenty-one, respectively. They have coincidentally, over my years of reflection and writing about ADHD and Ritalin, allowed me through their comments and discussion a special access to the world of the children, now adults, who are featured in this book. I am proud of their achievements and moral sensibilities as they enter the very same young adulthood examined in *Remembering Ritalin*.

As my wife, Denise, and I begin our thirty-eighth year of partnership, I marvel at our achievement of raising our sons and sharing a productive, accomplished life together. I call our relationship a "work in progress" in acknowledgment that any long-term relationship demands attention and change. Her perspectives and values infuse the ideas of this book. I am also grateful for her efforts to keep my ego firmly grounded.

Having published three prior books, I have some experience with editors and publishers. I believe this makes my high esteem for Marian Lizzi, my editor at Perigee, and the publisher, John Martin, especially credible. They never wavered from giving me their maximum understanding and support for this project. I also appreciate Joan Matthews for her excellent copyediting work on the manuscript.

Susan Tasaki, my local Bay Area editor, is a true artist/magician—she regularly weaves my heavy clothes prose into crystalline gold. This is the second book we've worked on together. Her ability to clarify my ideas and words allows me a freedom and speed in writing that make us a terrific team. Her promise to meet deadlines in the face of other professional and personal demands was especially valued on this go-round.

I save my final gratitude to my long-term agent and friend, Beth Vesel. Fourteen years ago, she discovered me at the professional equivalent of "Schwab's soda fountain," and has since guided me through four books and several other professional writing ventures. We've shared the experiences of our children growing up and the world in which they live. This book is first dedicated to her.

CONTENTS

1

. . .

A Professional and Personal
Journey of Caring

"How are they doing now?" Sheila Comers wondered as she walked
into my office in May 2009 carrying a copy of *Running on Ritalin*, a
book I'd written thirteen years earlier. As a behavioral-developmental
pediatrician who evaluates and treats children with behavior and
learning problems, I had spent much of 1996 working on *Running
on Ritalin*, drawing on my case files for examples that illustrated the
controversies surrounding attention deficit/hyperactivity disorder
(ADHD) and the use of the drug Ritalin.

Sheila was interested in how the kids discussed in the book had
turned out because she was concerned about her own seven-year-
old son, Devin. During the school year that just ended, his first-
grade teacher had complained to Sheila several times about Devin's
problems with the "f" word. In my practice—which spans thirty-
two years and more than three thousand
children—I hear the "f" word quite a lot.   **"I wonder how
However, my "f" word has five letters, not   they're doing now."**

four, and comes up in virtually every teacher referral made to my office: *focus*, or lack of it, in the classroom.

After the teacher had tried verbal reminders and redirections, moved him to the front of the room, and sent him to the principal's office twice within a six-month period for being disruptive, she suggested to Sheila that perhaps Devin needed a medical evaluation. Both Sheila and the teacher knew well that "medical evaluation" was teacher-speak for finding out if Ritalin would improve Devin's classroom behavior and performance.

My "f" word has five letters, not four: *focus*, or lack of it, in the classroom.

Sheila was upset, though not surprised. At home, it was often a major battle to get her son to pick up his toys, end a video game, or complete his homework. Her husband, Frank, had fewer problems with Devin, though that may have been because he spent less time with him and rarely addressed the homework issue. He did, however, agree that an evaluation should be pursued.

During Sheila's search for medical practitioners who dealt with these types of problems in children, she found my website. She discovered that I'm an MD subspecialist who prescribes Ritalin but is committed to effective nondrug interventions, including behavior modification and special education services. She also noticed that I had written three books, and was intrigued by *Running on Ritalin*'s subtitle: *A Physician Reflects on Children, Society and Performance in a Pill*. Before we met, she checked the book out of the local library and read it, thus provoking the question with which she started our first session.

The publication of *Running on Ritalin* in 1998 propelled me to the forefront of a national debate on the use of psychiatric medicines in children. My participation in this debate was provoked by what I felt was an absence of legitimate criticism of the boom in the use of the drug, which began in the early 1990s. Among the most prominent Ritalin critics, Peter Breggin, an adult psychiatrist, challenged any use of Ritalin, which he described as a virtual poison for children's brains. His hyperbole and lack of clinical experience with children set him up as an easy straw man for the proponents of the ADHD diagnosis and Ritalin as its first-choice medical solution.

"Medical evaluation" was teacher-speak for finding out if Ritalin would improve Devin's classroom behavior.

My position was more nuanced than Breggin's—it wasn't black or white. As a subspecialist pediatrician who had prescribed Ritalin to children nearly every day of my then twenty-year practice, I still questioned the burgeoning use of this drug for more and more children. I was curious about a multiplicity of factors involved—genetics, children's personalities, their families and schools, the materialist American culture—in the social creation of an expanded disorder of ADHD. I was and remain relatively unique within the medical community in my public challenge of the predominant theoretical model of brain biology and chemical disorder that purports to explain all of children's behavior and school problems.

At the time, I was both surprised and gratified that my concerns resonated with so many others. It was exciting to appear on television talk shows and, later, to offer testimony to a congressional subcommittee investigating Ritalin use and give a presentation to the President's Council on Bioethics—especially since I was not a university-based research scientist but a frontline behavioral-developmental pediatrician with a private practice.

IS AMERICA STILL RUNNING ON RITALIN?

The broad social and cultural concerns raised in *Running on Ritalin* continue to this day. Indeed, with the explosive growth of the

ADHD diagnosis in children—and in adults as well—and the concomitant boom in the use of stimulant prescription drugs such as Ritalin, the questions raised in *Running on Ritalin* are even more relevant and timely now than when the book was initially released.

Why does the United States have 80 percent of the world's ADHD?

The questions about the ADHD diagnosis that comprise the book's core continue to be asked: Is ADHD a legitimate disease or a social construct to excuse poor parenting or lack of attention to children? Is it overdiagnosed or underdiagnosed? Why does the United States have 80 percent of the world's ADHD? Does it have something to do with what we eat or some pollutant, or is it the consequence of a fast-paced, overdemanding lifestyle? Or at the most personal level, has our anxiety over our children's feelings about themselves paradoxically led us to become intolerant of even their smallest deficiencies?

Now, thirteen years later, much has changed about the diagnosis and who gets it. There isn't (nor has there ever been) a biological or even psychometric marker for ADHD. Thus, in recent years, ADHD has become "gentrified"—children and adults with comparatively mild problems become candidates for Ritalin when performance is a problem in a critical area such as school or the workplace. Compared to a dozen years ago, diagnosis rates have exploded, but especially in the very young, girls, teens, and adults. Today, the "inattentive without hyperactivity" variety of ADHD predominates the diagnosis rates.

What about treatment for ADHD? How safe and effective are the pharmaceutical products used to address ADHD? Are there effective nondrug treatments? Why is it still easier to find a doctor who will prescribe a pill than one

Compared to a dozen years ago, diagnosis rates have exploded.

who will direct and support a behavioral intervention? Do any of the alternative or complementary treatments that seem to come and go truly make a difference, and if so, why aren't they supported by insurance or the government?

In *Running on Ritalin*, I examined organized psychiatry's role in the explosion of American ADHD, but I did not address the power of the drug industry. In 1996, the government's policy of linking medical research and teaching to for-profit drug and device manufacturers was only just beginning to have a major impact on my practice. That was also the year that Shire Pharmaceuticals introduced Adderall to our nation's doctors with the largest marketing campaign to date. The subsequent course of ADHD (the public's awareness and acceptance of the diagnosis) and its treatment (prescription stimulant drugs such as Adderall) constitute a prototypic "case history" of the industry's influence over society's views on children's mental health and illness.

Are there effective nondrug treatments?

Ritalin is the trade name for the generic chemical methylphenidate, which is nearly identical to the better-known amphetamine, a drug also used to treat ADHD. In terms of individual children, methylphenidate and amphetamine may have somewhat different effect and side effect profiles, but short-term outcomes for large groups of children are the same. Though Ritalin remains the best-known stimulant drug, others such as Adderall, Concerta, Metadate, Focalin, and Vyvanse (to name just a few), along with generic methylphenidate, long ago passed it in terms of sales in the United States.

A note on terminology. In this discussion, I use Ritalin as shorthand for the whole class of stimulant drugs. Similarly, unless I indicate otherwise, ADHD is shorthand for the group of attention disorders listed in the American Psychiatric Association's *Diagnostic and Statistical Manual*, 4th edition (*DSM-IV*). These include

ADHD-inattentive type, which technically is a very common kind of ADHD that does not include hyperactivity. Virtually everyone now calls this particular problem attention deficit disorder, or ADD, though the official terminology has not yet changed. There are some similarities (mainly in response to Ritalin) but a lot of differences in terms of the problems and causes of ADHD and ADD. In this book, when I feel it's important, I will make a specific distinction between ADHD and ADD.

RITALIN'S SHORT-TERM VERSUS LONG-TERM EFFECTS: MORE QUESTIONS THAN ANSWERS

Sheila wasn't just interested in fixing Devin's problems at school and at home. She also wanted to know what was wrong—what was causing Devin to act the way he did. She wanted to know whether he did or didn't have ADHD. Her online research indicated that ADHD was a lifelong disorder that could require Devin to take medication for the rest of his life, and she dreaded that. On the other hand, if that was what modern medical science determined, then she was prepared to follow through. The alternative, she told me, was to feel that she had neglected her son's medical needs— that she was a bad mother.

"I'm not sure what to believe," she said plaintively. "Online, there are such contrasting opinions about ADHD and the medicine." I could empathize. A parent perusing the general literature would find Ritalin portrayed as both a miracle drug and a potentially addictive brain poison. Medical literature, on the other hand—with a few dissenters—views Ritalin as a safe and effective short-term, first-choice treatment for ADHD.

She wanted to know what was wrong—what was causing Devin to act the way he did.

Unfortunately, the *long-term* benefits or downsides of drug treatments for ADHD are far less known and more controversial because of the dearth of studies and the absence of clear benefits for any of the childhood treatments—drug or nondrug. There have

"Online, there are such contrasting opinions about ADHD and the medicine."

been thousands of studies on the short-term effects of the medication; most of this research has studied the drug's effects on children for a period of eight to twelve weeks.

In addition, hundreds of studies have examined the current and previous lives of people initially diagnosed with ADHD as adults. But perhaps only four or five studies have followed children for decades. Virtually all long-term (formally termed prospective or future-oriented) studies of ADHD and Ritalin have methodological problems that make it possible for the conclusions to be wrong, or at least not accurately predictive of a child's future, on or off medication. Parents are usually shocked to learn that although millions of children have been prescribed stimulant drugs, doctors really don't know the long-term effects of the medications.

There are many reasons why there are so few studies. Primary among them is that studies require researcher dedication, longevity, and, most importantly, money. Since the early 1980s, most drug studies have been funded by private industry. Because laws governing the release and marketing of prescription drugs require only three months of proven effectiveness and safety compared to a placebo, there is little profit incentive to study these drugs long term. In fact, there may actually be *disincentives*, particularly if the drug proves to be ineffective or otherwise problematic.

Furthermore, over the last three decades, the bar has without question been lowered in meeting the criteria for what constitutes behavior definable as ADHD. This means that behavior that today is defined as ADHD would not have been defined that way in 1990.

There is little profit incentive to study these drugs long term.

So even if individuals with and without ADHD were tracked for twenty years, it still might not be possible to know exactly what's in store for Devin. It's probably safe to say that his predicted outcome won't be worse than that of boys diagnosed in 1990.

Finally, it's important to distinguish who is diagnosed and followed in the university-selected samples that are the basis for the long-term studies on ADHD and medication. There's a big difference between cases of ADHD discovered in the community or the general population versus those children whose families go to a university center for evaluation and treatment. The university-sample children will have worse symptoms that have not responded to local community practitioners such as pediatricians or even first-line specialists like me. Major university medical centers such as the University of California, San Francisco (UCSF) or Stanford University Hospitals are last-resort institutions in the San Francisco Bay Area, for example. This is also where research in ADHD is conducted.

Also, at least one of the parents of the children I see has a job. With a minimum of one parent employed comes the necessary medical insurance or income sufficient to pay for the services of a private medical doctor. The large university centers, like UCSF or Stanford, must by their charters treat all comers, with or without the financial means. Families with fewer economic and social resources are concentrated in the centers that do the research on ADHD. Thus, children with severer problems coming from poorer families constitute the primary research population. These are some of the reasons to question the applicability of the long-range studies for children of parents now reading this book.

Nevertheless, what, in general, do the few available university studies tell us about people now in their mid-twenties and thirties who were originally diagnosed fifteen to twenty years ago? The news is grim. Up to one in three of these younger adults continues to meet criteria for the psychiatric disorder of ADHD. A little more than half finish high school. Only one in ten completes four years of college. They have much higher rates of substance use (particularly alcohol and marijuana). Much higher arrest records. More car accidents, more divorce. The list goes on. The medication they took for years in childhood possibly ameliorated some of their symptoms through their adolescence but had no effects lasting into young adulthood.

Notwithstanding the studies' weaknesses, the research verdicts are clear. ADHD continues at least through the first three decades of life, and ADHD sufferers continue to experience significant employment and relationship impairments. The research states (or implies) that medication into adulthood may make a long-term difference, since most of these individuals generally stopped using the medication sometime in their teenage years. But researchers also acknowledge that this thesis is speculative.

Up to one in three of these younger adults continues to meet criteria for the psychiatric disorder of ADHD.

Sheila was aware of the research. She, like many parents I've seen in my practice, hoped that Devin didn't have ADHD, but would be both relieved and resigned if he did. At least then she would know the cause and could make choices about treatment. From my perspective, the ADHD diagnosis is clear only for a minority of hyperactive children. From what I could tell from her account of Devin's behavior, he was only mildly overactive and impulsive. Yet in my experience, it was still quite possible that even with mild symptoms, Devin could wind up taking Ritalin for years.

"I just think sitting at his desk for six hours at school is too hard for him at this time."

At her core, Sheila had trouble believing her son was destined to be a drug-using dropout and criminal. "He has such a good heart," she told me. "I just think sitting at his desk for six hours at school is too hard for him at this time." I silently agreed. Sheila had intuitively concluded what I have sensed over my three decades of working with children with attention or impulsivity problems. Over the years, I've learned how some of my former patients were doing (twenty-plus years ago, many more boys than girls were diagnosed with ADHD; this trend continues, albeit with a narrower margin between the genders). With only a few exceptions, most were okay to well: They were students, taxpayers, not on medication or abusing substances. I wondered why I wasn't hearing about the same bad outcomes as frequently as were my university-based colleagues.

I've come to believe that children who go to frontline community-based specialists are not as severely affected and that their families have better resources than children included in the studies. For years, I've said that I've seen more of the Tom Sawyer/ Pippi Longstocking variety of ADHD. But I don't kid myself—most doctors in the United States today would diagnose both Tom and Pippi with ADHD and put them on Ritalin for several years at least.

But I also have to wonder whether or not my ideas about ADHD and my approaches to its treatment were significantly different from even the presumed "state-of-the-art" treatment offered at university centers. My nondrug approaches have always been to focus on helping the parents become more effective, especially with discipline. And I've made advocacy for the children at their schools a primary intervention. I wonder how many Individualized Educational Plan (IEP) meetings—in which educational and behavioral strategies for the child are decided in concert with the teacher and parents—the researchers attended. There is a place for Ritalin in my practice, but only after these other efforts have been given a good chance to succeed—and have failed to sufficiently help the child at school or at home.

Sheila's question triggered an idea of my own. What if I systematically tracked down some of the children whom I treated in 1996? I knew that my follow-up efforts would not meet any rigorous scientific criteria. My research would be personal, as seen by only one physician, lacking consistent psychometric data and direct comparison to a control group of children without problems.

Nevertheless, my follow-up would reflect an ADHD diagnosis sensitive to the cultural milieu in which it was made. The pressures on kids, their teachers, and their parents to perform have grown tremendously over the past twenty years as many of the supports have declined—the economic need for both parents to work full-time among them. My research into a socially aware ADHD diagnosis and an emphasis on first employing nondrug interventions for treatment is just not comparable to the "scientific" studies that use a *DSM*-symptom-based approach to the ADHD diagnosis and a medication-first approach to ADHD treatment. The readers of *Remembering Ritalin* can decide which type of study is more useful in making decisions about their children today.

> My follow-up would reflect an ADHD diagnosis sensitive to the cultural milieu in which it was made.

I felt that finding out more about my former patients and how they were doing would be of interest to the larger group of parents (and children) who are treated at the community level. My hypothesis was that their outcomes would not be as bad and would offer hope to the families whose children take Ritalin today. I wondered if today's twenty- and thirty-year-olds—the first group of what's been called Generation Rx—could also benefit by hearing from others who shared their experience.

I thought, too, that it would be both fun and interesting to do this follow-up. Doctors who specialize in children only occasionally learn of good outcomes. Children and their families who continue to have problems and/or require medication are obviously followed for a longer period of time—sometimes into early adulthood. Otherwise, there is the occasional encounter on the street and the even rarer intentional contact by a former patient or parent to thank me and tell me how well things had gone.

WHY REMEMBER RITALIN: A MORE PERSONAL ANSWER

So, this covers the official "why" of this book. But as I thought a bit more about this project, I also realized that writing *Remembering Ritalin* would be the continuation of a personal journey that began almost twenty years ago. In the early 1990s, after a dozen years of practice, I first encountered what I later recognized as a profound shift in the culture, a shift that precipitated a professional-personal disconnect. To better understand this moment of stress, which I briefly touched upon in *Running on Ritalin*, you should know a bit more about me.

Neither I nor anyone in my family has ADHD. Some say this condition must be experienced firsthand to truly understand it. I suppose such could be said about any problem. Yet it's my job as a professional to try to understand all points of view. Let me be very clear that, despite any criticisms I might have about the diagnosis, I completely believe there is such a thing as ADHD and ADD. There is a small group of children and adults whose brains are "wired" differently. These people have very serious problems with self-control, impulsivity, and attention. I also believe they constitute less than one-tenth of the children and adults who take Ritalin-type drugs in this country today.

While I believe that ADHD is real, I deeply distrust the overall tendency to label individuals with this diagnosis. This skepticism is based on my professional evaluation of the science of ADHD, but it also represents something more personal. With few exceptions, scientists rarely write about the ways their backgrounds or personal histories have shaped their professional attitudes. However, I think these personal stories are important to acknowledge, since they often play a role in shaping scientific theory. Though we believe our theories are fact-based, neutral, and impersonal, in reality they are also influenced by who we are. And I am no exception.

I completely believe there is such a thing as ADHD and ADD.

All doctors, despite claims of objectivity, have a personal agenda inextricably tied, consciously or unconsciously, to their professional beliefs, theories, and practice. Here, I examine my personal feelings, beliefs, and history. You will learn the basis of my biases and the sources of my personal agenda—at least as well as I know them myself at this time. This is my attempt at truly "informed consent" and addressing, as best I can, any hidden psychological "conflicts of interest" when speaking to you of ADHD and Ritalin.

In my case, I have a distinct personal reason for my professional criticisms. The experience of my Jewish parents, Holocaust survivors, has given me reasons to be deeply worried about professing "the truth" about another person. It has also made me hyperaware of the danger of labeling or defining an individual or a group of people.

I do not, of course, equate having ADHD with being Jewish in

With few exceptions, scientists rarely write about the ways their backgrounds or personal histories have shaped their professional attitudes.

Europe during the 1930s and 1940s. Nor does my unease with labeling unite me, as some have interpreted, with "antipsychiatry," a movement that peaked in the 1960s, which claimed that all mental illness was merely a social fabrication. I will reiterate here, once again, that I believe ADHD *exists* and that biology, genetics, and brain chemistry are critical but not the only factors in the development of children's behavioral and emotional problems. Yet I continue to have concerns about the short- and long-term disadvantages of categories that both simplify and limit descriptions and beliefs about a person. I was turned off by traditional psychoanalytic psychiatry during my medical school training for a variety of reasons, among them its penchant for labeling children with pathological diagnoses.

More than thirty years later, mainstream child psychiatry now subscribes to a genetic, chemical, brain-based theory of children's maladaptive behavior (ADHD, obsessive-compulsive disorder, bipolar disorder, and so forth). They have thoroughly dismissed the theories and practices of the Freudian analysts. Yet the doctors of this new biologically based psychiatry promulgate a similar pathological diagnostic system that labels children, albeit now with presumed biological disorders. Even worse, these new "disorders" bring with them an aura of science, something that the old Freudian labels could only aspire to.

As an intern in pediatrics at the University of California, San Francisco, in the mid-1970s, I was fortunate to train under Helen Gofman, MD, a pioneer in the field of behavioral-developmental pediatrics. Among her instructions to her trainees: "It is better to describe your patients than give them a label." Her approach was a much better fit with my scientific and emotional outlook, and I went on to do my pediatric behavioral-developmental fellowship at UCSF's Child Study Unit under Helen's tutelage.

"It is better to describe your patients than give them a label."

WHAT'S IN A NAME: *DSM-III*'S LIMITATIONS

My distrust of the psychiatric diagnosis was heightened in 1980 with the publication of the *DSM-III*. Its authors attempted to improve psychiatry's standing within the American medical community by completely distancing this version from the vague and ill-defined disorders of the previous editions. *DSM-III*'s diagnoses were to be based solely on symptoms, not causes. With this change, the role of context in the creation and perpetuation of symptomatic problem behaviors was eliminated. This change turns out to be a crucial *deficit* of its own when considering children's ADHD-type behavior and its treatment.

When I talk to parents, I explain the role of context by using a toddler's sorting toy, a box with a lid and three-dimensional plastic objects, usually a cube, a ball, and a pyramid. The lid has three holes in the shape of a square, a circle, and a triangle. The child's challenge (and fun) is to match up the object with its corresponding hole and push it through and into the box.

In my analogy, I say that children's personalities and talents come in various shapes and sizes, as represented by the three-dimensional objects. Doctors who rely primarily on the *DSM* are evaluating only the objects. I, on the other hand, believe children's problems emerge not from the "shapes" of their personalities and talents alone but from the effort required to force these unique shapes through the mismatched spaces in the container's (or life's) lid. In real life, these spaces represent the demands of school, family, and peer relationships, among others. In other words, it is not the shape of the objects themselves that is the problem, but rather the friction generated when those objects cannot easily be pushed through the openings.

It is not easy to change personality or temperament. Some would, in fact, say that these qualities are inherent and unchangeable. However, can the way a family functions be changed to help the child cope more successfully? I believe it can, and have seen countless parents change their previously rigid ideologies and expectations of their children. For example, "He *can't* do it" is a common belief of parents who think their child has a disorder. If they can alter their belief to only "It's *harder* for him to do it," then they can adapt their parenting styles and strategies to the needs of their child's particular personality and be more successful (without drugs).

Similarly, most experts believe that developmental and learning strengths and weaknesses are biologically based. Special education theory and techniques are the indicated response to these presumed biologically based learning disorders. However, there's a controversial, rarely publicized secret about special education: It has never proven that it can change the basic abilities of children. Returning to my sorting toy analogy, special ed helps by changing the shape of the educational hole a child must fit into—it changes expectations about a child's performance and offers extra help and more individual instruction.

When efforts such as parent counseling and special education fail to change the holes of societal expectations and responses, Ritalin (or another drug) is the next tool to come to mind. I see Ritalin acting as a kind of lubricant that allows these differently shaped children to slide more easily through a specific expectation hole with less friction and resistance and, therefore, fewer problems.

Diagnosis by *DSM* does not take into account the societal (family and school) expectations for and responses to children; it merely counts symptoms. If children have six of nine criteria behaviors (for example, fidgets a lot, talks excessively, leaves his or her seat, doesn't pay attention, is easily distractible, doesn't follow through, or procrastinates) for either kind of ADHD—the hyperactive or ADD-inattentive type—they meet criteria for the diagnosis. The unstated implication of the diagnosis is that the problem is now considered chemical and brain-based and justifies medicating the child, perhaps for the rest of his or her life.

I have always strongly objected to this reductionist view of children's behavior. Apart from the stereotyping it engenders, it fails to acknowledge the role of families, schools, and society in general. The notion that the problem lies solely within the child bothers me greatly, both from a practical treatment point of view and ethically. By raising issues of context, I do not mean to say that parents or schools cause ADHD and are therefore to blame. But I do firmly believe that to be both honest and ethical, a diagnosis of ADHD must take into account the role of parents and the expectations of schools.

THE NEW "ADHD EPIDEMIC"

I think context explains best why the rates of ADHD and Ritalin use have soared in the last twenty years. In *Running on Ritalin*, I attempted to explain this phenomenon circa 1996. Among the countless societal factors behind the epidemic was our obsession with our children's performance, especially in school. There has been a pervasive ratcheting up of expectations of learning and self-regulated behavior in the classroom.

Children in public school are now routinely expected to read

Children's brain development is the result of hundreds of thousands of years of evolution and cannot change because of a thirty-year cultural shift.

at age five, one full year earlier than thirty years ago. Multiplication and division have also been moved up by one full year. Children's brain development is the result of hundreds of thousands of years of evolution and cannot change because of a thirty-year cultural shift. Many children will be able to adjust to the new demands, but a large segment cannot and are diagnosed with ADHD.

Our confusion about discipline and children's self-esteem has left teachers and parents uncertain how to handle children's misbehaviors. Conversation about feelings and rules are in. Active rewards and punishments (especially punishments) are out. Children, more and more, are expected to figure out how to behave on their own. A large group, especially young boys, need more action and fewer words to help them stay in control. Without a confident, active authority figure to direct them, many of these children will need Ritalin to stay in control.

The results: In the last thirteen years, already high prescription stimulant rates grew by astounding margins (see the postscript for details). Today, at least one in ten eleven-year-old boys take Ritalin equivalents. The diagnosis of ADHD among adults has increased exponentially. The use of prescription stimulants in adults has likewise exploded—some college campuses report that more than one-third of their students have used these drugs legally or

Some college campuses report that more than one-third of their students have used these drugs legally or illegally.

illegally, either for power studying or getting high. Rather than a disease or disorder, ADHD has become a personality type or lifestyle. Ritalin is no longer a treatment for a specific problem, but a universal performance enhancer that has been compared to a steroid for the brain.

Young adults routinely talk of the benefits of "multitasking." Someone forgets to do something and says, "Oh, that's because of my ADD," whether or not they've been for- mally diagnosed. Doctors, lawyers, corpo- rate leaders, and others with undeniably high achievement still feel they have ADHD

ADHD has become a personality type or lifestyle.

when they become overwhelmed with aspects of their work. They then go to ADHD specialists, who routinely give out the diagnosis along with performance-enhancing stimulant drugs.

They are many "urban legends" about Ritalin. Among the most ubiquitous is that somehow Ritalin, a stimulant, works differently in the hyperactive mind to slow both the child's activity and im- prove concentration. In fact, studies have shown over and over again that amphetamine-like drugs in low doses (not at abusing lev- els) have the same effect on everybody. They improve concentra- tion and make people more deliberate. As you increase the dose, concentration actually deteriorates and people (including children with ADHD) act speedy and nervous. (See Chapter 10 for more on this and other urban legends.)

Another myth about Ritalin is that it improves complex thinking. It doesn't. Ritalin is hardly a "steroid" for the brain, as some have recently touted. However, when you are on the drug, you *think* you're doing much better than your actual performance. Perfor- mance on repetitive or mundane tasks does improve. You'll be able to stay up all night to write your college paper, but the quality of that work will be suspect. However, if you didn't take Ritalin, you might not have done the paper at all.

Later in this book, I will explore these phenomena in detail and address both the pros and the cons of the Ritalin explosion. But for now, I'd like to return to the issue of context as it relates to children. Over the past thirteen years, my thoughts on why we use so much Ritalin with our children have matured. Society's obsession with performance may explain Ritalin's popularity, but it doesn't fully explain why increasing numbers of children are being prescribed not just Ritalin but all types of psychiatric drugs.

I used to believe that it was our fear of our children's falling behind or failing, especially in school, that drove the ADHD/Ritalin craze. The same drives that had parents drilling their kids to get into the right preschool, prep for the SAT, and hire professional consultants for college applications was, I thought, fueling the Ritalin explosion. Higher education and a degree from a good college were the best guarantees for economic success—read "happy" life—for their children.

But now I've come to believe that the causes for the Ritalin boom go beyond just our concerns about our children's performance. I now think our love and our anxiety about our children's feelings, especially their self-image or self-esteem, drive both the Ritalin and the children's psychiatric drug boom. Rightly or wrongly, we worry so much about our children's feelings—especially if they feel bad about themselves—that, ironically, we've become less tolerant of minor variations in their performance and behavior. We worry greatly about how they fit into those holes I mentioned earlier, and the effects the friction has on them.

We worry so much that when our initial efforts to help them are unsuccessful, we're quick to take them to the doctor. In our culture, the doctor's role is to make diagnoses using the *DSM*, usually followed by a prescription to treat the newly diagnosed condition. And of course, teachers' concerns, doctors' business practices, drug companies' influence on medical research, doctors' professional education, and direct advertising to parents also influence the decision to use Ritalin. However, I strongly believe that pills, while potentially

> We worry so much about our children's feelings . . . that, ironically, we've become less tolerant of minor variations in their performance and behavior.

effective, are not equivalent to addressing factors in a child's environment.

PILLS VERSUS ENGAGEMENT: THE ETHICS OF INTERVENTIONS

But love and worry about our children paradoxically narrow the spectrum of what we consider to be normal behavior and make us more inclined to view them as having disorders and needing medication. Yet does labeling kids with disorders and giving them drugs for years make the most sense when dealing with their differences? What happens when these children grow up? Do these interventions make a difference in the long term? Are pills still necessary when an individual gets to choose the hole to fit into? My hypothesis was that as my ADHD patients matured and had choices about where and how to apply their talents and interests, their perceived need for medication would decline; except for the most severely affected, few would be taking the drug in their mid-twenties. As I began this project, my hope was that my research would confirm this hypothesis and offer hope to parents whose children currently struggled to fit into the metaphoric rigid holes of that children's sorting toy.

Once again, to be clear, I've never been against prescribing psychiatric medications to children. At the same time, I have long recognized that giving a child a pill—even one that worked and was relatively safe—was not the same as helping that child with non-drug-based treatments. Pills emphasize efficiency, while attention and actions require caring engagement.

I do not judge parents who ultimately decide to use medication for their children's problems. Many parents are not offered effec-

Do these interventions make a difference in the long term?

Pills emphasize efficiency, while attention and actions require caring engagement.

tive alternatives; certainly, after attempting unsuccessfully to address a child's problems without medication, the impulse to try anything that works is understandable. But I also have a very hard time remaining silent when I see that, under the guise of science, a less ethical approach to helping children and their families is being offered first—or is the only alternative provided by doctors and other professionals.

This may also be related to my personal background. During World War II, the Allies were silent and took no action as the atrocities of the Holocaust in Europe became well known. I'm not sure if my parents' connection to this history has led me to feel that silence or inaction in the face of clear ethical impropriety is unacceptable. But in any event, it is unacceptable for me to remain silent about the social and cultural pressures when children with minor performance or behavior problems are diagnosed with mental disorders and then prescribed drugs without a thorough examination of their individual situations or without a strong commitment to nondrug solutions.

That being said, after I've attempted to address a child's problems with nondrug interventions, I continue to prescribe Ritalin, even to children with minimal ADHD. I do this because in the end, I don't believe Ritalin is a dangerous drug for children (its abusive addictive potential in adults is a real threat and another story). I also believe Ritalin and other similar drugs can help children in the short run. However, there is no doubt in my mind that I prescribe more Ritalin to children because there are social and cultural factors at work that overall are deleterious to children's health.

Do I leave these kids to struggle without medicine even if factors unrelated to the child's behavior—families with two working parents, unrealistic school demands, limited nondrug intervention opportunities—have contributed to their problems? I've resolved this ethical conundrum with my commitment to acknowledge and attempt to change these contributing conditions while at the same time prescribing drug therapy to help children and families cope. This two-pronged approach addresses my own moral quandary while offering a sensible solution for many children who fall into this all-too-common category.

WELCOME TO THE "RITALIN WARS"

This moral compulsion to speak out about conditions that hurt our children has put me in hot water. Like most people, I prefer to be liked, and it's difficult when some of my opinions, rightly or wrongly interpreted, anger others. I think in particular of the ongoing differences I've had with Joseph Biederman and his colleagues at Harvard's Pediatric Psychopharmacology Clinic in Boston. I will say more about Dr. Biederman and his travails later in this book, but for the moment, I recall his power and vitriol when, in 1998, he publicly dismissed *Running on Ritalin* in a presentation I happened to attend.

I've thought long and hard about the vehemence of the criticism I've received over the questions I've raised. Joe Biederman wasn't alone. The national leadership of the leading self-help organization, Children and Adults with Attention Deficit/Hyperactivity Disorder (CHADD), invited me into a private session during their annual conference in New York in 1998 and proceeded to grill me for ninety minutes over *Running on Ritalin*. There were whispers that Diller was a publicity hound, interested in just selling books, getting on TV, and making money.

> This moral compulsion to speak out about conditions that hurt our children has put me in hot water.

These imprecations also hurt. I've come to realize that the ADHD diagnosis and Ritalin remain, despite academic and self-help efforts otherwise, controversial. Both groups, by the way, receive major funding from the pharmaceutical industry—prescription stimulants earn greater than $2 billion annually. Thus, when a professional insider like me challenges the perceived orthodoxy, it is taken as a grave threat to a towering but internally unstable edifice.

To add fuel to this fire, the media tend to exaggerate and oversimplify some complex issues about ADHD and Ritalin. These repetitive passion plays in the print and electronic media have been colloquially referred to as the "Ritalin Wars." Like it or not, I knew I would be enlisted in the antimedication camp, even though I prescribed Ritalin virtually every day I'm at the office.

There are Diller detractors and then there is leadership that has been open to dialogue. Russell Barkley, arguably the architect of the modern ADHD movement worldwide, may debate with me publicly on TV the merits of the diagnosis and Ritalin treatment, but privately, we have had many productive exchanges. I know he shares many of my concerns about the trivialization of the ADHD diagnosis.

Similarly, Sam Goldstein, a human dynamo and clearinghouse of information on ADHD and its treatment, and editor of the *Journal of Attention Disorders*, has had me on the journal's editorial staff as its book editor since 2004. It's a marvelous position for me not only to review the professional and lay literature on ADHD, but also to influence the debate by selecting which books to review and having the power to invite a reviewer of my choice to write the review.

So I have my critics and supporters. Notwithstanding either, it continues to be important to me to raise issues and consciousness about ADHD and Ritalin. The alternative is to remain silent and participate in a medical and social process that I judge to be less than ethical and moral for children. For me, this silence is worse than any criticism or censure I might arouse by speaking out.

"HOW ARE THEY DOING NOW?"

Back to the question originally posed. I was curious how the children of *Running on Ritalin*, now young adults, felt about the treatment they had received. In 1996, long-acting stimulants were not available; any child who needed assistance with school in the afternoon, or later in the day for homework, would have to take a second dose at lunchtime and possibly even a third at home. How different or stigmatized had they felt by having to take medication? Did they feel the medication was helpful, and if so, in what ways? How did they feel about side effects? Did they always tell the doctor the truth about how they were feeling? Did they recognize the efforts of their parents and teachers to help them in other ways? Which interventions did they value more, then and now?

Thus, I, too, wondered, "How are they doing now?" To answer that question, I needed to track down the children of *Running on Ritalin*. I hadn't closely reread the book's case histories for several years and wasn't certain I'd be able to identify all the children, whose names and related data I had changed to protect everyone's privacy.

But I had clear memories of virtually all these children. Steven Gordon was six in the first grade and an inveterate daydreamer. There was Deke, the mildly autistic two-year-old, whose activity and limit testing drove his parents crazy. Four-year-old Johnny Hestor's parents were more memorable than he; I still painfully recall his mother, overwhelmed by her job and family demands and unsupported by her husband, walking out of my office never to return because I suggested we try a behavioral plan before giving him Ritalin.

My focus, however, was on those children who had been slightly older, at least eleven or twelve in 1996, because now they would be in their mid-twenties. I arbitrarily chose twenty-four as the minimum age of follow-up. My sense was that, socially and culturally, by that age most of their adolescent issues (the identity crises, rebellion, intensity, and erratic behavior normal to teens) should have eased, and if not would constitute lifelong problems for these kids.

Jenny Carter, a sensitive, quiet fourth-grader with a slower cognitive style, would now be twenty-four. Sam Maynard, now twenty-six, had a complicated history that included anxiety, ADHD, social awkwardness, and tics; he took Ritalin as well as several other psychiatric drugs. How would Bobby Hall be doing now? He was twelve when I wrote *Running on Ritalin*, but I had known him since age seven as one of the most hyperactive children I had ever met. I prescribed Ritalin for him for eleven years, but once he left high school, I no longer heard from him.

Jim Hassler was sixteen when I first met him. He had been a straight-A student, but he and his parents felt he couldn't do it without Ritalin. He also "came out of the closet" during our time together. He'd be thirty-four now. I used Kevin O'Rourke and his family to illustrate how medication for ADHD might not be enough when discipline was awry. His adult life had been unhappy, and I was very interested in talking to him if he would talk to me. He was now twenty-eight.

I didn't think it would be too hard to track down these kids. I've been in the same place—Walnut Creek, California, a middle-to upper-middle-class suburb east of San Francisco—for thirty years. I have always maintained detailed written clinical records on my patients and, for medical and legal reasons, have kept them. I also have financial records on my patients from that date. So it seemed that most of the kids from *Running on Ritalin* whom I could identify by their real names were still in one set of records or the other.

What's more, given the ages of the kids I intended to contact, nearly all of them would be using Facebook, the web-based social networking system. And indeed, using either their names or sometimes their siblings' names, I rather easily tracked down an email address for a number of my former patients or someone in their family. My hope was to do face-to-face interviews with all of these now grown-to-young-adulthood children and perhaps talk to their parents as well.

In the chapters that follow, I use these long-term stories to highlight the issues parents, children, and society continue to face with regard to ADHD and medication. The next chapter reviews and critiques in more detail the results and problems of the main academic studies that have followed children into young adulthood, especially the landmark work of Russell Barkley.

Chapter 3 features Sam Maynard, who as a twelve-year-old was diagnosed with a number of disorders and labels, none of which fit him well. Sam's story illustrates how the diagnostic criteria for ADHD have changed over the years. Chapter 4 asks, "Is ADHD really the problem?" Though frequently, impulsivity and inattention are presenting concerns, they are often the result of some other stressor, particularly learning or family problems. We'll find out how dreamy or anxious girls are doing at age twenty-five.

Chapter 5, "Living with ADHD: Finding the Right Job," focuses on Evan, who struggled with learning problems all the way through high school but then had the drive and wisdom to go to a two-year auto mechanic training program instead of community college. Cameron also struggled in school and tried community college for a year before dropping out. Now he thrives with a multiplicity of several self-created jobs and is on the way to earning his "first million," as he puts it. Both took stimulant medication for years. Evan still does.

Chapter 6 follows up on Bobby Hall, the very hyperactive kid who was on Ritalin for more than a decade. In talking to Bobby, I learned that the most painful aspects of ADHD as he was growing up were not his problems at school or at home. Rather, Bobby felt he never fit in, and was terribly lonely in middle and high school. This chapter focuses on peer social relationships and ADHD, which may be the most important problem for the ADHD child today.

Not all outcomes are positive. In Chapter 7, the main focus is on Kevin O'Rourke, whom I'd known since he was seven, and his family. Kevin, like Bobby, was among the most impulsive, hyperactive children I had ever met. At the time I wrote *Running on Ritalin*, he was thirteen. With the help of an excellent special high school program, Kevin managed to cope. But after his parents separated and divorced, he went to live with his father. His tragedy will be explained and its roots, in retrospect, analyzed. We also meet Daniel, who as a teenager seemed destined to follow Kevin's track; at twenty-four, his situation appears much brighter.

No book on the long-term outcome of ADHD and Ritalin would be complete without a look at the risks of alcohol and legal and illegal drug abuse, especially stimulant abuse, in adulthood. Jim Hassler was sixteen when I first met him and now is thirty-four. In Chapter 8, his experiences with numerous legal medications and some illegal drugs illustrate the confusing, conflicting promise and fears about Ritalin use in children. Katie, at thirty-one, appears on the surface to be moving ahead with a successful art career. Yet she remains unhappy, struggling with herself over success and the meaning and risks of Ritalin. All of these young adults were aware of the surge in the illegal use of prescription stimulant drugs such as Adderall by their contemporaries.

Chapter 9 explores what ADHD and medicine mean to us today. How have things changed—or not—in the more than a dozen years since *Running on Ritalin* was written? Are they better or worse? How important does ADHD remain for the young, middle-class adults included here? Last, I consider how I have changed my ideas about my role in that time. What have I learned about my effectiveness and limitations by following up with these patients and their families?

Many parents who read this book will be in the same situation as Sheila, who started me on this quest with her query. Young adults questioning their own lives may also wonder if they have ADD and need treatment. Parents want to know the long-term outcomes, but they also want to know how to go about getting adequate evaluation and treatment for their children. Today, there are even more expensive but still-unproven diagnostic and treatment strategies than there were thirteen years ago; three decades in the ADHD biz, and I'm still waiting for the big nondrug breakthrough. When it comes to the alternative and complementary medicine scene for ADHD, the more things change, the more they stay the same. So, in the final chapter, I offer a potpourri of observations on what my thirty years of clinical experience have confirmed and debunked, as well as a walk-through guide to self-diagnosis and life and career choices for young adults. The postscript to *Remembering Ritalin* leaves us with data that should raise major concerns about the overall direction our country is heading with the use of performance-enhancing drugs.

From my point of view, most of the relevant long-term social and economic trends I noted in *Running on Ritalin* continue to hold sway. Though at times I have felt very discouraged, I continue to speak out. In 2005, I was buoyed when the FDA hearings that highlighted the alarming number of suicides among children on Prozac grabbed the attention of the public and the government.

The hearings began a cascade of exposures that cast a harsh light on physician conflict-of-interest scandals in academic medicine. With the adverse publicity, the pro-brain/pro-drug science has come under renewed scrutiny and skepticism. With all this negative publicity, people are no doubt even more confused about ADHD and Ritalin now than they were in 1996. What we discover in *Remembering Ritalin* will assist us in finding what we need to know about our children and ourselves in the twenty-first century.

2

. . .

ADHD Children Become Adults

What the Science Says—and Doesn't Say

Ever since the reorganization of American medical schools a century ago, there's been a gulf between frontline practitioners (like me) and doctors who perform research and teach at medical universities. As though to reinforce this gulf, we have disparaging terms for one another. I'm an LMD, or a local medical doctor. When I was a medical student at Columbia and pediatric resident at UCSF, the LMD acronym used in the presentation of patient histories implied that care had been inferior, idiosyncratic, non-science-based, or all of the above.

However, as I moved from medical center to private practice, I quickly discovered a complementary denigration of the university-based physician: the "ivory tower doc." This connoted a doctor whose ideas and practices were impractical, inefficient, unrealistic, and, in particular, non-cost-effective for operating in the "real world" of office medicine. The theories and suggestions offered at teaching seminars and in journal articles might be of interest, and could indeed have some influence on the progress and value of medical practice. But except in those rare circumstances in which dramatic results were obtained, change would be slow to come to the generally skeptical, experienced frontline practitioner. I thought of this long-standing gulf between researcher and practitioner as I dialed the number for Russell A. Barkley, PhD.

MAINSTREAM RESEARCH ON CHILDREN'S OUTCOMES WITH ADHD

Psychologist Russell Barkley is universally considered to be the intellectual father of modern ADHD. From the time he began working with the problems of childhood hyperactivity in the mid-1970s, his research, writing, and advocacy over the past thirty-five years have had a profound influence on the practice of pediatrics and child psychiatry. His authority and renown are based on the rigor of his specifications and standards in studying these children and their families. By the 1980s, he had amassed a body of published work on the subject, and while other researchers were also working in this field, his criteria for what constituted the disorder most closely matched subsequent standards for ADHD. One could deduce, in fact, that his criteria were the primary source for the 1980 *DSM-III* standards that revolutionized official psychiatry's view on hyperactivity.

Barkley was not interested in treating children with interventions that were felt, but not proven, to be helpful. Rather, he sought solutions that could be verified and replicated. Almost thirty years ago, he assembled groups of similarly affected children, which he compared to nonaffected children from the community. He then followed the course of both groups, monitoring treatments and outcomes. His most recent data and conclusions are set forth in the book he coauthored with Kevin R. Murphy and Mariellen Fischer, *ADHD in Adults: What the Science Says*.

Barkley and I came of age professionally toward the end of the reign of Freudian theory and practice on child psychiatry. Like me, he rejected the limited and rigid model that posited that children were born

Barkley considers ADHD to be a specific brain-based biological disorder.

as blank slates to be influenced by their parents, especially their mothers. That's where our overt similarities end, however.

Barkley considers ADHD to be a specific brain-based biological disorder; he also maintains that ADHD can be precisely defined, and has created and set standards that have had international influence on the way this condition is perceived. While I have repeatedly acknowledged a neurological-biological component to the problem, I also emphasize children's temperaments acting within the context of a variety of demands and responses from the environment. The problem of children's behavior is, for me, relative and less absolute. Since I am a frontline clinician, my primary goal is to improve the problem situation, regardless of what it's called, for the child and family.

As I admitted for myself in Chapter 1, I suspect that personal factors also influenced Barkley's mission. He has written quite openly about his troubled fraternal twin brother, whom he believes was affected by ADHD his entire life. Tragically, his brother died in 2007 while driving under the influence. One cannot help speculating how, consciously or unconsciously, Barkley's family-of-origin relationships have molded his work on this topic.

MEDICINE VERSUS NONDRUG APPROACHES: THE OPENING ROUNDS

My first public encounter with Barkley came in 1996 with an exchange of letters published in the professional magazine *Psychiatric Times*. He had written an important article commenting on the early findings from the Multimodal Treatment Study of ADHD (MTA), a major government inquiry into ADHD and Ritalin. It involved more than six hundred carefully selected children who had been diagnosed with ADHD, and was intended to be the best and most definitive study ever of the condition.

As Barkley was one of the principal investigators, he was privy to these results. Thus, backed by the authority of the study, he could write that Ritalin was the definitive treatment for ADHD. Even in 1996, I was troubled by the implications of a medication-first approach to the problems of ADHD and, in my letter, contended that Barkley's conclusions might actually harm children by diminishing the importance of parenting or educational interventions. (As it happens, the study's initial conclusions, which were based on the findings of its first two years, were strongly tempered over the subsequent eight years of follow-up.)

A couple of years later, at a national meeting of ADHD's primary self-help organization, Children and Adults with Attention Deficit/Hyperactivity Disorder (CHADD), Barkley gave a keynote presentation to an audience of several thousand. I vividly recall his restating the multitude of biological, genetic, familial, psychometric, and behavioral evidence that supported his position. In firm tones that brooked no dispute, he said, "This is a disorder, this is a disorder, this is a disorder!" He pounded the lectern using his closed fist with each "disorder." His passion, precision, and power were impressive, and when he finished, the entire audience rose in unison to cheer and applaud. I remained seated, feeling awkward and wondering why I was so uneasy with his speech and its reception.

Over the course of the next ten years, Barkley and I were regular opponents in professional and lay magazine articles. We must have appeared at least a half-dozen times on television or panels, taking different sides of the ADHD medication debate. Finally, knowing that we were to take part in yet another panel discussion in front of the American Psychological Association in San Francisco, I invited him to meet me for a drink after the session. To my surprise and pleasure, he accepted. During our conversation, I learned that one-on-one, Barkley was quite charming (and liked Grey Goose vodka). But more importantly, I discovered that our privately shared views on ADHD and its treatment were far more similar than what we espoused in public.

Since then, when I have had a major question about ADHD, I've contacted Barkley, who has always made himself available or answered my queries quickly. For example, he and I have extensively discussed ADHD in adolescents, and I used that conversation as the basis for an essay that was included in my book *The Last Normal Child*. Now, I wanted to speak to him about his formal research into adult ADHD. I was particularly interested in trying to figure out why the children of *Running on Ritalin*, now young adults, appeared to be doing much better than the cohorts of ADHD children included in his studies and in those of most of the other researchers in the field.

FORMAL LONG-TERM ADHD STUDIES: THE VERDICT

As I also mentioned in Chapter 1, I didn't intend my informal follow-up to meet the criteria of a scientific study. Still, the contrast between the published literature on adult ADHD and the young adults I contacted for this book is stark. While there have been thousands of studies on children with ADHD, only five have followed them into young adulthood.

If one considers the millions of children diagnosed with ADHD who have taken Ritalin-type drugs, the number followed into adulthood is strikingly small: 103 in Montreal, 101 in New York, 50 in Sweden, and 158 in Milwaukee—four studies that Barkley considers worthy of consideration in his book on adult ADHD. A fifth study (of 179 boys) from Irvine, California, merits mention, but its inclusion criteria and focus (highlighting ADHD *and* oppositional behavior, or children who repeatedly challenge adult authority) were not as specific for ADHD as the other four. I mention the Irvine study now because I will refer to it repeatedly in Chapter 7 ("Bad Outcomes"). I did, however, choose to concentrate on the children in Barkley's Milwaukee study. Without a doubt, this group had been the most extensively assessed via a panoply of physical and psychological examinations. More studies have been published about this cohort than any other comparable group. Barkley captured, in great detail, their outcomes approximately twenty years later; he also ably makes the case that his findings are generally consistent with the smaller studies mentioned above.

In 2009, before I began writing this book, I read a summary of Barkley's research on ADHD children in adulthood in the *Journal of Developmental & Behavioral Pediatrics*. His analysis of his research data delineated in great detail how ADHD remains a lifelong disorder, with significant impairment into adulthood. Here are some of the outcomes he included in his article:

- In terms of impairments (most to least), education, home responsibilities, and occupational domains are the most functionally impaired in adults with ADHD.

- Academic retention (30 percent), academic tutoring (50 percent), special education classroom placement (30 percent), and/or dropping out of school (10 to 35 percent) are all relatively common academic consequences of ADHD.

- Young adults with ADHD completed fewer years of education, with nearly one of three failing to complete high school. Similarly, other studies have reported that relatively few young adults with ADHD attempt college (20 percent), and even fewer (5 percent) graduate.

> **Over half of all adults with ADHD are likely to have been fired from their jobs.**

- Occupationally, children with ADHD are at risk for having significantly lower occupational status in adulthood. Adults with ADHD have a lower socioeconomic status than siblings without ADHD. Over half of all adults with ADHD are likely to have been fired from their jobs.

- Adults with ADHD may also have problems related to maintaining health-conscious behavior. Less than half of all adults with ADHD exercise frequently (compared to 65 percent of community controls).

- Trouble sticking to budgets, exceeding credit card limits, failing to pay for utilities (resulting in termination), being in debt, and going on shopping sprees are reported (in excess) in those with adult ADHD.

- Adults with ADHD are more likely to have received a speeding citation, had an at-fault accident, and had their license suspended or revoked.

- Individuals with ADHD are likely to initiate sexual activity earlier (one year earlier on average) and engage in riskier sexual activity (more partners, less use of contraception). Teenage pregnancy and sexually transmitted diseases are also more common in adolescents with ADHD.

- If married, adults with ADHD self-report a lower quality of their current relationship, and are more likely to have extramarital affairs. Parenting stress is also reported to be significantly higher in adults with ADHD.

Between 75 and 80 percent of adults with ADHD have an additional psychiatric disorder.

- Between 75 and 80 percent of adults with ADHD have an additional psychiatric disorder.

- Conduct disorder and oppositional defiant disorder occur in 24 to 35 percent of clinic-referred adults with ADHD, which is lower than the rates reported in pediatric ADHD (50 to 60 percent). One-third of all children with ADHD have been in jail at least once by the time they reach young adulthood.

- Alcohol dependence or abuse disorder prevalence rates range from 21 to 53 percent.

- Between 16 and 31 percent of adults with ADHD have also been seriously depressed.

The list seemed all bad. While I hadn't followed up on my patients in any formal fashion, over the years I had heard about them, often casually at my local Italian delicatessen, where I'd bump into one of them, or their parents. While we waited to order, I would learn who was in college, where they were working, whether they were still living at home. Most importantly, I wasn't hearing the breadth and depth of negative outcomes that had been informally believed and circulated about childhood ADHD among professionals, and which these just-published, long-term studies were now confirming. I was puzzled, and curious; perhaps it was something as simple as people being reluctant to share negative outcomes while waiting in a line for a sandwich. Still, they looked and seemed happier, healthier, and more connected than mainstream research indicated was likely.

I wasn't hearing the breadth and depth of negative outcomes.

When I interviewed ten of these young adults for this book, my "findings" were far more positive. At the time of the interviews, these kids ranged in age from twenty-four to thirty-four. Only one had been jailed, and while only four had finished college, another four had graduated from an alternative post–high school degree program such as art school or certified automotive repair training. Only one appeared to have a substance abuse problem. Though none was legally married, one had fathered a child, and half were in long-term relationships. Only two were taking a Ritalin-type prescription drug. (I will be sharing more of the details of my "cohort" in subsequent chapters.)

In essence, my delicatessen-based assumptions were confirmed by talking in depth to my former patients and, in some cases, to their parents. Why, then, were my outcomes so much better than those quantified in formally based research? I could flatter myself and say that I was a better doctor, but I don't believe that's the case. An alternate explanation is that the researchers performed "bad" science. I don't buy that either. These scientists were topflight and dedicated, using the most sophisticated assessment and follow-up tools of their time. There clearly must be another explanation.

THE "NATURAL" COURSE OF CHILDHOOD ADHD

Before calling Barkley, I pored over the mass of statistics in *ADHD in Adults* and prepared a list of questions. When we finally spoke, I suggested that the differences in outcome between his group and mine had to do with the children in his study and those I saw in my practice. He told me that the children recruited for the Milwaukee study met a "research criteria" for ADHD that later fit well into the *DSM-III* criteria (published in 1980). "In fact, the children probably had more severe symptoms than the current *DSM-IV* permits, especially for the inattentive type," he observed.

While at the Milwaukee Children's Hospital, Barkley recruited children ages four to twelve for his study. "Milwaukee Children's, where we ran our clinic, was not a tertiary care center [like today's Harvard or UCSF clinics]. This was the 1970s. Most of the area pediatricians were part of the staff. However, we were the only clinic dealing with hyperactive kids in Wisconsin. The neurologists didn't want them. Our children [the ADHD and matched normal controls] drew mostly from the area, which *economically was lower, lower-middle, and middle class* [italics added]."

In this study, Barkley undertook a mammoth task: to clearly delineate the parameters of ADHD and establish it as a legitimate, biologically based disorder. "We attempted to impose categories over what are clearly dimensional symptoms. The line is arbitrary. But at the end of the day, we are treating harm. The question is, to what extent." In other words, Barkley was saying that the symptoms and behaviors such as inattention or hyperactivity vary significantly in the community from not at all to very much. And the decision to declare a certain greater degree of a disorder and the rest variations of normal is difficult and potentially quite arbitrary. I may add that Barkley and I generally agree on which kids "have" ADHD. We also agree that the diagnosis has been applied with little justification in many cases. And I would agree with him that in certain populations (for example, inner-city African-American or rural), significantly impairing ADHD goes undiagnosed.

> "We attempted to impose categories over what are clearly dimensional symptoms."

After his time in Milwaukee, Barkley set up an ADHD research center at the University of Massachusetts Medical School in Worcester (a tertiary university medical center), at which he maintained and ran an ADHD specialty clinic for self-referred adults—people who thought their problems might be caused by ADHD. In addition to the need for treatment, this population gave Barkley a perfect opportunity to collect information on those who met his criteria for the adult version of ADHD and who may have been missed as children.

But these adults, whom he calls the "UMass group" in his book, were clearly different from the Milwaukee children. For one, the Milwaukee children didn't refer themselves; their parents did. The UMass adults thought they had an ADHD-associated problem. Clearly, this group of adults was unhappier with their situations than members of the general population who didn't go to psychiatric clinics. This is known as "referral bias" (or bias toward more disease or impairment) and is an unfortunate consequence of the economic realities of running a long-term study.

In order to avoid the negative bias inherent to a self-referred teen or adult clinic population and still generate statistically significant results for the population at large, Peter Jensen, the child psychiatrist who was in charge of the government's MTA study, calculated that at the start of such a study, one would have to include at least five thousand children from a representative *nonreferred* general population. These children would each have to have been evaluated for ADHD and then all of them followed for the requisite minimum of twenty years to get "unbiased" results.

It is unlikely that such a study will ever occur in this country. In the meantime, the best information on long-term outcomes and adult ADHD comes from those such as Barkley's. To his credit, in *ADHD in Adults*, Barkley separates the details of the outcomes for the Milwaukee and UMass groups. However, in his overall conclusions, he tends to conflate the generally poor results of the two groups. "For the most part, adults with ADHD that has persisted from childhood are remarkably similar to clinic-referred adults newly diagnosed with it" (*ADHD in Adults*, page 454). But as I studied his data, I wasn't convinced, in part because, within the Milwaukee group, one of the subgroups fared much better. The more I thought about it, the more I realized that this group's outcomes seemed to more closely match the adults I include in this book.

"RECOVERING" FROM ADHD

Barkley, in his analysis of the Milwaukee children at a median age of twenty-seven, found that 44 percent still had ADHD, 36 percent had "recovered," and 20 percent were subsyndromal—they still had signs of the disorder that resulted in significant impairment but did not meet his full criteria for ADHD. In his book, he designated those in the first and third groups H+ ADHD and those in the second group as H– ADHD. As I repeatedly scanned the tables of data and selected out the H– ADHD group, I invariably found that they were doing much better than either the H+ ADHD group or the UMass group.

Of course, this makes sense, because there is an element of circular or teleological reasoning in the diagnosis of ADHD.

> Since there is no biological marker for the disorder, the disease is defined only by its symptoms.

Since there is no biological marker for the disorder, the disease is defined only by its symptoms. If you don't have the symptoms, you don't have the disease, and if you do, you do. Critics of the ADHD diagnosis regularly invoke this problem in logic. In the extreme, the criticism is employed to conclude that ADHD doesn't really exist. While there is some validity to the criticism of the logic, it's clear there are children (and adults) who are highly impaired by behavior we call ADHD. But it does make definitions and criteria highly problematic.

I thought that the vast majority of my small group of kids fit within either the recovered or subsyndromal group. Only two of my follow-ups were still taking a Ritalin-type drug at the time of the interviews. Eight of the ten were full-time students or had jobs (though not all were self-supporting). While only about a third of Barkley's original Milwaukee group was H– ADHD, I judged that approximately 80 percent of those in my group were doing "well enough." The outcome of only one of the ten young adults I interviewed was clearly bad in my estimation.

In *ADHD in Adults*, buried in the mounds of data, I noticed some "interesting" factoids on the community controls from the

Milwaukee study—in particular, their responses to questions of antisocial behavior as adults. From the Milwaukee community group (those never diagnosed with ADHD), 45 percent said they had stolen property, 28 percent stole money, 33 percent had been arrested, and 24 percent jailed (at least once). Apparently the H+ ADHD group had to be pretty bad in this arena to statistically beat out their local norms.

My theories centered on the differences between the population from which the Milwaukee group was selected—inner-city Milwaukee in the late 1970s—and my population of patients, focused around Walnut Creek, California, in the mid-1990s. Fifteen years earlier, when casting about for a place to open up a private practice in behavioral pediatrics not far from San Francisco, I chose Walnut Creek, a suburb about twenty-five miles east of San Francisco. A middle- to upper-middle-class community, its families would have jobs that included medical insurance or would be able to pay out of pocket for specialized care. Over the past thirty years, Walnut Creek and the Highway 680 corridor have grown exponentially and are now dotted with pockets of wealth reflecting the vibrant San Francisco Bay Area economy.

MIDDLE-CLASS ADHD

When we spoke, I pointed out these numbers to Barkley, who was quite aware of them. I asked him if he felt the different populations in our "studies" could explain my better outcomes. "Absolutely. Your families likely had better resources. The families were more intact. The children probably had fewer comorbidities."

Barkley's last point was important. By "comorbidities," he meant that in large studies, the majority of children with ADHD also have other major behavior or performance problems. The two most important and more common are learning problems and oppositional behavior. The latter can lead to teenage conduct disorder and anti-social personality disorder. There is a group of experts who've surmised that ADHD alone isn't the big problem for children and their families; rather, ADHD in combination with these other difficulties leads to bad outcomes.

We speculated about the families of the children in Walnut Creek, and their environment in general. "It's probably both genetic and environmental," he said. By the former, he meant it's generally well accepted in the scientific community that by age twenty-five, children are very much like their parents (these conclusions are drawn from exhaustive studies on adopted identical twins who are reared apart). In all the families of the children I followed, at least one parent was working. Amazingly there was only one divorce, and even in that case, the parents appeared to have reconciled and were living together at the time I interviewed their son. Compared to the Milwaukee group, my families were not only biologically favored (they had characteristics that work positively in an industrial technological society) but also had more resources (among them, stronger familial connections; access to better schools, tutoring, and counseling; and better medication management) to help their children.

In Barkley's study, at age twenty-seven, the H– ADHD group's data on impairments were about the same as their community-matched controls who had never had ADHD. An area where Barkley's H– ADHD group still had problems was in the realm of education—lower rates of achievement, and of starting and finishing higher education. I noticed the same outcomes with my kids. Only four of these young adults had finished a standard four-year college program; most of the others had not even attempted to do so. Rather, they obtained alternative post–high school education in the arts, or more blue-collar professions such as automobile repair or law enforcement. Though these may not be the types of jobs to which those who feel that college degrees are required for a satisfying life aspire, they seemed happy in their career paths.

COMING TOGETHER ON ADHD CHILDREN'S OUTCOMES

Talking with Barkley relieved some of my concerns about my thesis. My findings were consistent with a minority subgroup of his study. Perhaps my outcomes were "too good," but I also felt that many of Barkley's groups' poor outcomes (as well as those of other studies that also drew from lower- to middle-class populations) could be explained by characteristics of the general population from which he obtained his ADHD patients.

Barkley's standards, interpretations, and opinions have been spectacularly successful.

I believe that Barkley's mission was, from the outset, different from mine. His cause was to define and make "real" ADHD and its biological and genetic components. Though my ideas about other, more personal reasons for Barkley's direction are speculative, his standards, interpretations, and opinions have been spectacularly successful. Worldwide, society has come to recognize ADHD as a "real" disease with biological roots that can be addressed by medical intervention.

Barkley has, perhaps, been too successful. I know that in recent years, while still flying the ADHD banner, he has expressed concern over the ever-expanding criteria, the misuse, the generalization, and, ultimately, the trivialization of the ADHD diagnosis. Toward the end of our conversation, we talked about this issue. "We run the risk of both over- and underpathologizing ADHD," he said. "On one hand, we have *The Gift of ADHD* [a book that purports that ADHD has benefits and value], which I just don't believe in at all. But otherwise, we can scare the hell out of people. Really, it's the minority of ADHD kids who go to jail. It is ADHD within the context of the family that makes it either very important or unimportant."

Hearing this surprised and pleased me; in our previous conversations, I had come to believe that this was how he felt, but had never heard him express it so clearly. He went on to say, "I can discuss these nuances with you over a drink. In public, our stands are more black and white. In reality, we should go through the fabric of the disorder and use our clinical judgment. You can't apply these findings as universals. The findings have to be applied within the context of the individual and his family."

It was a great relief to hear this; part of me always wonders if I'm crazy to hold the views and opinions I do on ADHD, because, in public at least, I'm considered to be in the minority. The uninformed think I'm against medication, which is completely incorrect, though I *am* against medication as a general first line of offense when other nondrug interventions for ADHD have not been tried. So it was very affirming for me to have this level of exchange with Barkley. I told him how appreciative I was that he was willing to take time to discuss this. "I like to be challenged by you," he said as we closed. "I don't mind these discussions at all."

Given my concerns about the continued growing use of psychiatric drugs in children with ADHD, I strongly suspect Dr. Barkley will be hearing from me again.

> "It is ADHD within the context of the family that makes it either very important or unimportant."

3

. . .

ADHD: A Protean Diagnosis

Sam Maynard is now twenty-six. Even though all the adults I interviewed gave me permission to use their real names, for the sake
of consistency I'm employing the names I used for this person and
all the other children in *Running on Ritalin*, now adults, to whom I
spoke for this book. Sam was eleven and a half and in the sixth
grade when I met him in 1995. I used his story in *Running on Ritalin* to highlight some of the limitations of the ADHD diagnosis
as defined by the then-current official criteria of the *DSM-III*. As I
began working on this book, I reread my file on Sam and was reminded that before I even met him, his mother, Susan, had sent me
a two-and-a-half-page, single-spaced "summary" of Sam's problems,
which began in the first grade.

Here's what I wrote about Sam in *Running on Ritalin*:

*He tended not to finish his work at school, instead switching his
attention to things he liked doing, such as building with Legos or*

working on art projects. His grades weren't bad—Bs and Cs—but he was clearly bright and capable of more.

Mildly impulsive, he was less of a problem at home, though often he would not do as his parents asked unless his father became quite stern or even physical. He generally ignored his mother, though not in a mean or spiteful way.

Sam had developed a throat-clearing habit that would wax and wane but never go away completely. It seemed to worsen when he became tense—if his parents were fighting with each other or yelling at him. He also sometimes demonstrated repetitive hand-wringing; this also increased under stress.

Sam complained about some vague, confused and troubling thoughts that he couldn't get out of his head. They might be what he called "bad" ideas or even inoffensive words that somehow disturbed him. He called these his "patterns."

Where Sam's problems most interfered with his life was in making and keeping friends. Though his language skills were okay, he was socially awkward and often misread social cues. His poor eye contact didn't help. He could usually latch on to one or two kids in his class who were also "different," but he ached for more friends.

I met Sam and his family at a time when parents weren't able to go online and check various websites for diagnoses and treatment. Still, Sam's mother was very sophisticated, and offered me at least five possible diagnoses for her son: ADHD, OCD (obsessive-compulsive disorder), ODD (oppositional defiant disorder), TS (Tourette syndrome), and AS (Asperger syndrome).

He had already been on several medications, including Tegretol, an antiepilepsy medication, which was prescribed following an abnormal electroencephalogram (EEG) even though he never clearly had a seizure. In addition, he took Dexedrine, a stimulant drug, for his ADHD and Anafranil, technically an antidepressant, but in Sam's case, employed to treat his "patterns." He had also tried clonidine (also called Catapres), a blood pressure medicine that is used in child psychiatry to treat ADHD as well as to suppress the tics of Tourette syndrome.

Though a child on four different psychiatric drugs before age eleven is still unusual today, it was practically unheard of in 1993, which was when I first met him. His story made me immediately think that his parents were both deeply caring and pretty anxious themselves. My hunch was right in that Susan, the *generalissima* of this family, relentlessly searched for new information, new cures—anything to help her son, for whom she had both deep love and worry. Her husband, Tom, was more skeptical of the whole process but also more exasperated with his son.

In *Running on Ritalin*, I detailed my experience with Sam up through the beginning of 1997. I stopped the Anafranil, which was making him quite tired, and switched him to Prozac, which was easier to take and had a solid reputation for helping children with anxiety (more effectively than for its marketed antidepressant action). He was no longer taking the Tegretol; it also made him tired and hadn't really changed any behavior (lesson learned: don't treat an EEG, treat the behavior). I also changed him over from Dexedrine to Ritalin three times a day (long-acting stimulants were not available until 1999) because I think Ritalin is slightly easier to take. Ritalin is methylphenidate, a variant of Dexedrine, which is amphetamine; amphetamine causes slightly more tension and irritability than methylphenidate. Finally, I switched him to Tenex (guanfacine), a longer-acting version of clonidine to address the tics of his Tourettes. However, none of these drug changes seemed to make a meaningful difference.

I suggested that Susan step up, demanding more from Sam and rescuing him less. Tom's job was to be a bit more patient and to spend more positive time with his son, as well as to take better care of himself (his job was very stressful; my notes also reminded me that Tom had had his own bout with depression, and took Prozac for a while). And in the beginning, I met with Sam almost weekly, working with him on eye contact and social interaction with other children. Ultimately, I didn't feel any of these strategies was particularly successful. I watched Sam's mood and his parents' reactions worsen through middle school. Eighth grade was the worst time for him. Sam, though quite isolated and sad, somehow mustered enough motivation to just pass his classes.

> **I watched Sam's mood and his parents' reactions worsen through middle school.**

Then, just as I was finishing writing about him for *Running on Ritalin*, he and his parents decided to take a big gamble. His brother, Joe, four years older than Sam, had had much success attending a small Christian school known for its strict rules and high academic standards. As I wrote in *Running on Ritalin*, "Sam wasn't their usual kind of student, but the director was sympathetic and willing to give him a try, with some special accommodations to his needs."

Sam seemed to blossom at the private school. In my last file entry of 1997, I noted, "Very solid start . . . despite some early detentions and check marks. In office he seems much more collected and competent, without any tics." I was guardedly optimistic about Sam's prospects at this new school, and it did seem to agree with him. Obviously, there were multiple factors; being permitted to follow in his successful older brother's footsteps meant a lot to Sam. The smaller class size and increased structure probably also helped. But Sam told me the main difference was the kids. He felt the children were nicer—better behaved and more in control of themselves (or perhaps, more controlled). He felt less intimidated, less picked upon. He was also older and out of the social cauldron known as middle school. He found a circle of friends.

My clinical notes continued to mark Sam's progress during his high school years, during which both his grades and his mood improved. By his sophomore year, he was taking college-level math classes and earning the respect of his teachers and peers. Then he decided to try going off all his meds. I didn't hear from him for almost a year, at which point he returned at Susan's behest after receiving some Cs and Ds on his report card. I restarted him on Dexedrine Spansule (a preparation that lasted up to eight hours), which he took through the end of high school.

My last notes on Sam are from 2000 and 2002. In July 2000, I wrote, "Sam is doing generally well. Grades improved from Cs and Ds to As and Bs, mostly by doing more of his homework." Ironically, the medication probably had nothing to do with the improved grades if the improvements stemmed from the fact that Sam was doing his homework, as the drug's effects only lasted through the school day. "He is interested in a four-year college. Susan reports increasing maturity based upon his own experiences as the way Sam learns about life." A note from 2002 has Sam asking me to document his earlier ADHD so as to facilitate his transfer to one of the state universities as a junior.

A MATH BRAIN SEEKS RELATIONSHIPS

And that was the last I knew of Sam until the fall of 2009, when I called his mother. Susan answered the phone and was very warm. She told me Sam was going to graduate school in Texas and immediately gave me his cell phone number. Next, I phoned Sam and explained my project. He was quite willing to speak with me, but since he was in Texas, we decided we would wait until he was home for his winter break to get together for lunch and talk in detail.

We met at my office the week before Christmas. As I greeted him in the waiting room, I was startled by the change in his appearance. Sam was now a stocky young man, about six feet tall, with a slight paunch. In meeting these young men whom I'd known mostly as adolescents, I was repeatedly struck, not so much by their height, but by their girth. All of them seemed to have filled out immeasurably. Some were well built while others, like Sam, seemed overweight. I remembered all of them as slight youths, even during their late adolescence. Some of their physical changes were developmental—the typical filling-out of muscle and mass twenty-something men undergo—but I couldn't help but wonder if taking stimulants like Ritalin and Dexedrine had kept their weight down throughout their childhood.

Sam wore a blue collegiate sweater and his hair was trimmed to almost military shortness, but he had several days' growth of scraggly beard. When he greeted me, he gave me good eye contact but I noted some blinking/twitching movement around his right eye, perhaps a vestige of his Tourette syndrome. Later, at the restaurant, I asked Sam what he remembered about coming to see me. "I wasn't listening to them [his parents]. I was having fights with my father. And then there were the effects of the ADD. I remember it very well."

When I asked him what it felt like to have ADD, he observed, "I'd have multiple things going on in my head at the same time, or I'd be daydreaming. It was a lot more interesting than paying attention to the real world. I wasn't so distractible. It was less about external things going on than about things going on internally with me." I noticed that his right eye was twitching excessively as he talked to me.

"I had fights with Dad. We were both very stubborn guys. It would start over something stupid and then we would both escalate.

Mom would try to be the voice of reason, but other times, she would leave the room." His memory was consistent with my own and the notes I had taken on the family dynamics.

I asked him about his compulsions, either his obsessive thoughts or rituals. He thought I meant the physical tics associated with the Tourette syndrome. "I had the sense that I really had to do it [the tics]. Maybe something bad would happen. I needed to do it or it would drive me crazy. I had to blink with one eye and then both."

I've tried to explain to others the "need" to blink, scratch, and yawn or whatever of Tourette syndrome. It's like the feeling most of us have had when we're getting over a bad cold and the only symptom left is a lingering cough. You're at a concert and feel a tickle and the urge to cough, but you try to suppress it until there's a break in the music. It gets harder and harder to hold back. Finally, the music stops. You cough and cough and it feels like such a relief—but for only a short time. Then the tickle begins again. Sam agreed with this description, but for him, there was also this vague nonspecific dread.

"I called my thoughts and actions 'patterns.' They could be paralyzing. It would slow everything down. Like, trying to get through a test was such a battle. I was also anxious that the patterns would make me wrong."

I asked him about other doctors he had seen before me. "I don't remember seeing doctors much. But I remember the meetings generally as tense and unpleasant. I remember my parents saying that they felt helpless and didn't know what to do. That made me feel very lousy."

"What do you remember about taking the medications?" I asked.

"I don't remember much about the Prozac. I couldn't tell if it was working or not. But the Ritalin—it did help me focus but it also seemed to have a depressing effect on me and my appetite. It got rid of some of the clutter, but at the same time, I felt lousy—not happy. I had some of my life sucked out of me."

Sam was not alone in his candor; others among my young adult interviewees spoke openly about their childhood dislike of being in the room with their parents when there were negative reports being made about them, as well as about the negative aspects of the Ritalin-type drugs. (Since my series of interviews with the young adults for this book, I've taken to asking children very specifically if they mind the flatness or the feeling of restraint. Interestingly, most of the preteens do not complain of this problem even when explicitly asked.)

When I asked Sam what else he remembered about the pills, he said, "I had to take [them] three times a day. It was a hassle having to go at the start of the lunch break. I'd rather be having fun. I didn't feel that different, stigmatized, or teased. But it was just the hassle of 'This is something I have to do.' I've always had a dislike of medicine. To me, it feels like a crutch. If other people can do without it, why not me? I valued it, but I also resented it."

"To me, it feels like a crutch. . . . I valued it, but I also resented it."

Sam took relatively short-acting Ritalin, which lasted only three to four hours per dose. In *Running on Ritalin*, I opened with a 1995 vignette of children lining up in front of the principal's office to receive their lunchtime dose of Ritalin. Some kids, like Sam, took a third dose when they got home from school. Concerta, which contains the same active ingredient (methylphenidate) as Ritalin, revolutionized the treatment of ADHD when it was released in 1999. An ingeniously designed capsule, it osmotically releases the drug from the moment it's swallowed to the point at which it's eliminated—up to twelve hours—and therefore eliminates the need for multiple oral doses. (Since Concerta was released, several other methylphenidate/

amphetamine preparations—Adderall XR, Metadate CD, and Vyvanse—all claim ten to twelve hours of action.)

Besides the hassle factor, Sam's other complaint about taking the medication was his feeling that it somehow made him different, less able as compared to other children. This almost universal feeling can usually be addressed in part by the way the drug and its effects are presented to children. By their teenage years, most children feel they are different from their peers. However, children with learning or behavior problems often face that existential issue at a much earlier age.

I asked Sam to talk about what I believed was his biggest challenge: his social problems. He explained in matter-of-fact fashion, "I was a geek, not popular. I had some really good teachers. But I didn't get along with the kids in my grade. I got along well with those one grade lower."

I reminded him about his last year in middle school, when he seemed so angry and sad. In fact, my notes suggested that he was bordering on suicidal, and I was quite worried about him at the time. "There was no particular low point," he said without emotion. "It got a little bit better towards the end. No one likes middle school. It's hell. Kids are mean at that age."

"No one likes middle school. It's hell. Kids are mean at that age."

It seemed to me that he'd managed to erase the worst aspects of that time from his memory, or at least wanted me to think he had.

He continued: "I stopped taking the medication in high school at the end of sophomore year. I didn't like the side effects. I wasn't happy and I had a decreased appetite. The thought of eating anything made me sick. I liked eating pizza but I couldn't. Then I'd be starved. It was no fun. I still struggled off the Ritalin. It did help."

Until I reminded him, he seemed to have forgotten that he went back on Dexedrine for the last half of his junior year and for apparently all of his senior year in high school. Then he stopped the stimulant and hasn't taken one since. "I went to two years of community college. It was still rough. I had two bad semesters, but in the third semester at DVC [Diablo Valley College] I got a 3.8 GPA. I got into UCLA by the skin of my teeth."

Sam talked about his transformation at the four-year college. "It occurred to me, 'Hey, I'm not at community college anymore. They're going to teach me what I need to know.' I took the responsibility seriously and did well. I despised LA in general, but UCLA . . . I loved every minute. It's a beautiful campus. There's a quality education there. I graduated cum laude. I didn't know so many of my professors were so famous. I like my independence. I'm responsible and that feeling only increased when I started paying my way in graduate school. It's up to me."

We discussed his friendships during his college years. "I kept some of my friends from high school. Two friends went to UC Santa Cruz and I would visit them while I was going to DVC. When I went to UCLA, I immediately hit it off with my roommate, and then there was a college Christian group I attended."

After leaving UCLA, Sam was accepted into graduate school at the University of North Texas. "My work is in descriptive set theory. There aren't a whole lot of schools to choose from. As it turns out, a lot of the UNT teachers were trained at UCLA. UNT is in Denton, about forty minutes from Dallas. It has over a hundred thousand people. My parents bought a house in Denton for me. I pay them rent."

Without my prompting, he then talked about a subject in which I was most interested. "I've been on only a few dates since I moved to Texas. I'm still shy. Yes, I'm a little bit lonely. It would be nice to have a girlfriend, but it's not too bad. I still feel socially awkward. Mom gives me a hard time about it. She would like me to do more. I belong to a Dungeons and Dragons club. I go to the movies occasionally. I'm not particularly physical, but I've started going to the gym to work off some weight."

"What about the ADD?" I was curious—he hadn't mentioned it at all. "Does it still bother you?"

"I still daydream some. Just a little bit. But I've gained some control over it. I'd consider taking Ritalin again except for its side effects." He volunteered that he was still on medication. "In October 2007, I started taking Zoloft. I'm up to 150 milligrams daily. It helps with my OCD. It puts me into a better mood—well, not that *much* better, really. It also helps me get off my obsessive thoughts."

I was a little surprised that he was still troubled by his "patterns." For years, people have mistakenly believed that the actions of selective serotonin reuptake inhibitors (SSRIs, among them Prozac, Zoloft, Paxil, Celexa, and Lexipro) were limited to improving mood, as in "antidepressant." SSRI users note that their experiences and reactions are more even and less volatile, without the feelings of sedation common with taking medications such as Valium, Xanax, or with drinking alcohol—other substances that also blunt sensitivity. So I asked Sam about this more universal effect of the SSRIs such as Zoloft: "Do little things bother you as much when you're on the Zoloft?"

"Not really. I wouldn't put it that way." Apparently, the mood effects were greater for him. I tried to be diplomatic when I asked him if he had experienced any of the sexual side effects common to SSRIs—decreased interest in sex and trouble ejaculating or reaching a climax. "Not really," he answered succinctly, though I wondered how many sexual experiences with others he had actually had.

I returned to the first problem he discussed and asked him whether the Tourette syndrome still affected him. "I still have an eye twitch. Sometimes I blink so hard I can develop a rash around my eye. I still play with my fingers some, but I don't take any medication for this problem."

As we reached the end of our time together, I asked him about his future. "I'm not sure I want to be a full professor who writes papers," he answered without hesitation. "You know, you write a hundred-page thesis on something that only two or three people might care about, and it really doesn't make a difference anyway. The job I'd like to get is working for the Department of Defense. I have a mathematician friend who works for them. He can't tell me what he does specifically, but he says it's great. That appeals to me more than teaching or writing—somehow my work making a real difference. I used to think that working on a problem for its own sake was enough. Now I want my work to matter to some degree, in a more meaningful way—no pure research."

Finally, I returned us to the main question I was interested in exploring. "So, overall, what do you think these days about taking Ritalin?"

"Ritalin for me . . . it wasn't a good idea. It did what it was supposed to, but the side effects were too much. I don't recall resentments. I know why they [his parents] were doing it. Your kid is hurting—you want to try to help."

I shared my theory on what made the difference for him: transferring from public school to the private Christian school. "Succeeding [there]—that was my golden goal." He wanted to follow in his brother's footsteps at the school. "My brother's now an MBA in Washington, D.C. He works for a British company. I got much closer to him when we were in high school for two years together. Now we're still close. I saw him with my parents in D.C. during Thanksgiving. He's not married either yet."

As we said our good-byes in the restaurant's parking lot, Sam shook my hand, and then as he moved away, he gently touched my shoulder; it was a very sweet gesture and I was glad we had reconnected.

THE "MULTIPLE PERSONALITIES" OF ADHD

In 1995, it required four or five psychiatric diagnoses to come close to accurately describing Sam's problems. No other realm of medicine uses the concept of comorbidity—qualifying for more than one diagnosis simultaneously—as frequently as psychiatry. The need for multiple diagnoses suggests a weakness in our basic system of using the *DSM-IV* (the most current version) to categorize children's abnormal behavior. The lack of a clear biological sign (anatomic, biochemical, genetic, electrochemical) for any psychiatric diagnosis is, in my opinion, the root cause for the often complex and highly subjective process of assigning multiple diagnoses to children.

Meeting with Sam and reviewing his history causes me to rate his ADHD as one of his lesser problems if we use his symptoms of impulsivity, inattention, and distractibility as measures. No doubt these behaviors were more of a problem for Sam, his parents, and his teachers when he was in elementary through middle school. But much changed for the better in the Christian school environment. Still, even in his last year of high school, he took Dexedrine because his performance and grades had declined without a stimulant drug—taken ostensibly for ADD, though these medications have the same capacity to improve concentration and focus for everyone (see Chapter 10 for more on this phenomenon).

If I had to decide which was Sam's most serious deficit, I would conclude that his struggles with his interpretation and response to the social clues of others—what we call today autistic spectrum disorders and which includes Asperger syndrome—continue to cause him the most frustration and unhappiness. Among the young adults I talked to for this book, Sam was not the only one who, for one reason or another, had relationship problems. Overall, I found that the quality and quantity of their social relationships outside their immediate families were the best indicators of how happy these people were.

• • •

By the time most of my former patients were in their mid-twenties, ADHD was either not a problem or was a minor one for all but two of the ten young adults I talked to. But just what, then, is ADHD? Can it be easily defined? Can we clearly say who does or doesn't have it? My short answer to the last two questions would have to be "no." I understand that my position flies in the face of the last twenty years of a vigorous educational campaign directed to doctors, parents, teachers, and even children, led by academic researchers and highly promoted by the drug industry. In academic circles, I've actually been accused of being a "diagnostic nihilist"—a high crime of thinking that implies that I don't believe that ADHD/ADD exists.

> I've actually been accused of being a "diagnostic nihilist."

As I've mentioned before, I do believe ADHD/ADD exists. I just think it's hard to define or justify in most of the children I see for problems of behavior or performance. Many children I see in my practice have similar kinds of problems—an excess of physical activity, impulsivity, and inattention—compared to other children of the same age (see "Diagnostic Criteria for ADHD" below). But only a small minority—I would guess about one in ten—displays these problems all the time and in all environments.

Diagnostic Criteria for ADHD

A. Either 1 or 2

    1. Six (or more) of the following symptoms of inattention have persisted for at least six months to a degree that is maladaptive and inconsistent with developmental level:

INATTENTION

a. Often fails to give close attention to details or makes careless mistakes in schoolwork, work, or other activities

b. Often has difficulty sustaining attention in tasks or play activities

c. Often does not seem to listen when spoken to directly

d. Often does not follow through on instructions and fails to finish schoolwork, chores, or duties in the workplace (not due to oppositional behavior or failure to understand instructions)

e. Often has difficulty organizing tasks and activities

f. Often avoids, dislikes, or is reluctant to engage in tasks that require sustained mental effort (such as schoolwork or homework)

g. Often loses things necessary for tasks or activities (for example, toys, school assignments, pencils, books, or tools)

h. Is often easily distracted by extraneous stimuli

i. Is often forgetful in daily activities

2. Six (or more) of the following symptoms of hyperactivity-impulsivity have persisted for at least six months to a degree that is maladaptive and inconsistent with developmental level:

HYPERACTIVITY

a. Often fidgets with hands or feet or squirms in seat

b. Often leaves seat in classroom or in other situations in which remaining seated is expected

c. Often runs about or climbs excessively in situations in which it is inappropriate (in adolescents or adults, may be limited to subjective feelings of restlessness)

d. Often has difficulty playing or engaging in leisure activities quietly

e. Is often "on the go" or often acts as if "driven by a motor"
f. Often talks excessively

IMPULSIVITY

g. Often blurts out answers before questions have been completed
h. Often has difficulty awaiting turn
i. Often interrupts or intrudes on others (for example, butts into conversations or games)

B. Some hyperactive-impulsive or inattentive symptoms that caused impairment were present before seven years of age.

C. Some impairment from the symptoms is present in two or more settings (for example, at school [or work] or at home).

D. There must be clear evidence of clinically significant impairment in social, academic, or occupational functioning.

E. The symptoms do not occur exclusively during the course of a pervasive developmental disorder, schizophrenia, or other psychotic disorder and are not better accounted for by another mental disorder (for example, mood disorder, anxiety disorder, dissociative disorder, or personality disorder).

CODE BASED ON TYPE:

314.01   ADHD, Combined Type: If both criteria A1 and A2 are met for the past six months

314.00   ADHD, Predominantly Inattentive Type: If criterion A1 is met but criterion A2 is not met for the past six months

314.01   ADHD, Predominantly Hyperactive, Impulsive Type: If crite-
          rion A2 is met but criterion A1 is not met for the past six months
314.9   ADHD, Not Otherwise Specified

Reprinted with permission from the Diagnostic and Statistical Manual of Mental Disorders, *4th Ed., Text Revision (DSM-IV). Copyright © 2004. American
Psychiatric Association.*

ADHD/ADD has also come to be seen as a neurobiological/
genetic/chemical disorder of the brain, even though no anatomical,
genetic, or biochemical difference has yet to be delineated. I, too,
believe that the behavior of ADHD/ADD has biological/genetic
roots, but then I also believe these factors contribute to all behavior: normal or abnormal, functional or dysfunctional.

Again, for a small group of children, neurological factors so pre-
dominate that it is easy to say, "They have ADHD." But they are
the minority. Most children in our country currently diagnosed with
ADHD are capable of sitting quietly and attending to subjects they're
interested in and, when not in school, can manage their behavior at
home with their families without requiring medication. Still, it would
also be wrong to say we are overdiagnosing ADHD if we pragmati-
cally consider that the Ritalin drugs regularly help these children
successfully cope with school demands.

The dilemma is that there is just no clear line separating the
majority of ADHD-diagnosed kids from other children who are
"normal," but very active or lively. In extreme cases of hyperactivity
and impulsivity, the diagnosis is made easily. But the symptoms of
ADHD in the general population range from the very focused to
the highly unfocused, with the large majority of children somewhere
in the middle of this bell-shaped curve. So, when one draws the line
between abnormal and normal, the majority of kids diagnosed with

ADHD/ADD will have to be of the mild variety, very close in behavior to those kids who don't have ADHD/ADD. Ultimately, where that line is drawn varies greatly with one's family, ethnic group, community, or culture. What doesn't change much are Ritalin's universal effects.

In extreme cases of hyperactivity and impulsivity, the diagnosis is made easily.

Furthermore, a person like Sam illustrates something that's true for everyone: We are not specific disorders. Our behaviors are too complex, too multifactorial in origin, too interactive within ourselves and with others to be reduced to a single descriptor: in this case, ADHD.

We gravitate toward simplification and reductionism—clear, yes-no answers. We think we then can know what's going on and how to treat it. Granted, many advances in medical science have been made by using this simplification (known as the medical model). A specific anatomic or chemical disorder leads to a specific treatment. But if we try to do this with ADHD, we wind up underappreciating the whole child and his or her interaction with the environment.

The diagnosis is attractive because it appears to also have a solution—Ritalin—though that answer alone is pejoratively known as the "quick fix." Our uneasiness about using medication as a first and only aid to children's problems lies with our sense that a pill, even when it works, isn't the moral equivalent to engaging the child with a more suitable environment. (I'll take up this issue in the last two chapters of the book.)

Back to Sam. His four or five diagnoses all potentially interacted to make his overall problems worse. His social problems (Asperger syndrome) could cause him to feel anxious or sad, which could make his ADHD, OCD, ODD, and TS worse. The impulsivity of his

ADHD could make social behavior and ODD more problematic. It's also very difficult to differentiate the "I don't want to" of ODD from the "He's disabled—he can't" of ADHD or OCD. And on it goes.

Finally, the nondrug interventions for virtually all of Sam's diagnoses were, in a broad sense, similar: developing a more immediate and effective discipline system while providing tangible rewards and privileges as incentives for good behavior and coping skills. Specific drug treatments are supposed to follow specific diagnoses, but in the real world of clinical practice, doctors generally choose the safest, most effective medicines first, such as Ritalin, before employing other drugs such as Prozac, Tegretol, clonidine, and so on. So do these diagnoses really matter? This is where I do begin to sound nihilistic, I suppose.

After three decades of working with children, I'm still not sure that psychiatric diagnoses are all that helpful in making pragmatic clinical decisions about drug and nondrug treatment. I don't care to be lumped together with the "antipsychiatry movement," which devalues psychiatric diagnoses for social or power-based reasons. My reasons are practical. In my practice, very, very few children behave in a way that is extreme *in only one* condition or disorder. The kids'

Very, very few children behave in a way that is extreme *in only one* condition or disorder.

behaviors may not even meet the full criteria of any specific disorder but may still have multiple symptoms that generate quite a problem for him or her and everyone else. I have no issue with declaring that a specific child "has" ADHD. But for most of the children I see—granted, few with as many problems as Sam—I prefer to describe the child and his or her environment rather than provide a label for a disorder.

For Sam, I would rather say he had SSD rather than the other alphabet soup of problems. What's SSD? Sam-specific disorder, of course.

THE HALL OF INFAMY

Brian Hanas wasn't one of my private practice patients. Rather, I worked with Brian and his parents, Carlos and Charlene, in the early 1980s while I was a fellow at the Child Study Unit at the University of California, San Francisco. He made a strong impression on me, especially since the encounters I had with him during those times left me with a profound appreciation for the power Ritalin can have on hyperactive behavior.

It had been such a long time ago, I had no contact information at all for Brian or his family. I thought I'd try Facebook, and to my surprise, I got a result, and an email address. I asked him via email if he remembered me from the Child Study Unit. He replied: "Don't remember you, but there were so many doctors." I followed up with a call to the number he provided; though he seemed vaguely suspicious and careful, he said he would check with his parents and get back to me. He was as good as his word, and I heard from him via email several days later. Brian said he thought it would be better for me to talk to his parents, as he really couldn't remember the details of so much that happened to him back then.

In *Running on Ritalin*, I included some of my observations about Brian from 1978.

> *All of seven years old, wiry and quick, Brian was one of the toughest kids being treated at the unit—a malevolent dynamo. I remember how his eyes darted around when, I imagined, he was planning his next caper. He often hit and kicked his parents during family sessions and dominated his larger (but more passive) older brother, Albert.*
>
> *One afternoon when I planned to see Brian alone, I went out to greet him and his father, but Brian leaped up and ran past me into*

the playroom. When I got to the playroom, Brian already had three boxes of toys down and their covers off. He lifted one box, dumped the toys noisily on the floor, spent a minute or two playing with them, then got up and dumped the next bin. "Brian, if you want to play with any more toys, first we have to put one of these bins away." He responded with a terse "Yup," but quickly started to build a tall structure, which he promptly destroyed. As he moved toward the third bin I stopped him and insisted he clean up some of the toys. Mechanically, but with little efficiency, he scooped up pieces and threw them haphazardly in (or toward) the bin.

To my questions about whether anything different had happened that day in school or at home, he responded in monosyllables, and kept on moving from one toy to the next. He couldn't stay with one for more than three or four minutes. Once he ignored my verbal warning, and I had to physically restrain him from trying to pull down a box that was too high. Finally, I gave him a time out—a few minutes on a chair to settle down (I too needed a rest)— but wound up physically having to keep him on the chair. After forty-five minutes I was drained bodily and emotionally, while Brian seemed even more wired.

Brian was among the most hyperactive and impulsive children I have met in my thirty years of practice. I have an informal internal system for categorizing the degree of difficulty a child's personality creates for him and others, based on levels of professional play in Major League Baseball. Some children's personalities are so easy they don't even make it into my professional league. Most of the children who come to my office have personality qualities that get them into the minor leagues. Those who are even more difficult make it into "The Show," as major league ballplayers call that level. The rare child (I usually treat only a handful of these at a time) is so difficult as to qualify as an All-Star. And finally, a few children—about two dozen out of three thousand—have made it to my Hall of Infamy. Brian was one of those children.

It wasn't Brian's degree of hyperactivity that gave him this unhappy distinction. He was also persistent and intense, and used these qualities to relentlessly test the limits and demands of his parents and teachers. In *DSM-IV* language, he also had a severe case of ODD. I've never particularly liked the designation of "oppositional defiant disorder"—I've always wondered, oppositional and defiant *to whom and over what*. Like the rest of the *DSM-IV* (and as best I can ascertain for the next version *DSM-V* due in 2013) diagnoses, the label is limited to the individual, but if there is ever a need to consider the parents' role, it's with this kind of child behavior.

Over the years, I had wondered about Brian's outcome. His parents were reasonable people, but reasonableness was in no way enough. Brian's challenges also exacerbated the differences between Carlos and Charlene. Carlos was a very laid-back, gentle man while Charlene was more of a firecracker. Charlene and Brian would butt heads, and Charlene would fume when Carlos didn't back her up sufficiently or take action on his own.

I and many other doctors believe it really isn't ADHD alone that causes problems in children. It's the ADHD in combination with other issues that creates the waves. Perhaps the most sinister combination is that of ADHD and ODD, which can morph, usually during the teenage years, into something more serious called conduct disorder, and then potentially evolve into antisocial personality disorder, which, in lay terms, means the individual engages in criminal behavior and spends significant time incarcerated. Some researchers feel that the combination of ADHD and ODD together should have a special diagnostic category of its own, because children who have both often have the worst outcomes, as Barkley and others' long-term outcome research has clearly demonstrated. But at least Brian was alive and his parents were still together. These facts alone were positive.

A THIRTY-YEAR-OLD THANK-YOU

It was with considerable interest and some trepidation that I waited as the phone rang at the Hanases' house. Carlos answered, and I identified myself; he remembered me, and said that Brian had mentioned my call. I explained to Carlos that I was doing a follow-up with patients I'd included in my first book, but Brian had suggested that I talk to them. He was amenable, but said he thought Charlene would be the better person to talk to. "She remembers more and can say it better than me." He handed the phone to Charlene, who must have been right next to him. It brought back thirty-year-old memories of the family, and how Carlos—a decent, good man but passive—generally handed over the parenting reins to Charlene, who was the more active, intense, and definitely more verbal of the two. I told Charlene that I wanted to find out how things had turned out for Brian.

"I'm so happy you called. After Brian told us you had contacted him, we've been thinking about you—just this afternoon. Dr. Diller, he got into big trouble for a while. After we saw you and Dr. Gofman [Helen Gofman, the director of the Child Study Unit], we went to the Longview Center in San Mateo. Brian's mind was so active—he never knew right from wrong. At twelve, he was made a ward of the state. It hurt us so to do it. But you guys saved his life. UCSF was so instrumental."

"What do you mean?" I asked.

"We were lost. We had no idea what we were dealing with. You were the first to explain to us what was going on with the ADHD. We thought we were just bad parents. It was still very hard, but you made it more tolerable. Ritalin played an important part. We had tried him on a few different drugs. We tried one drug and he was hallucinating for two days. The other medications put him into a zombie state. But more important than the medicine, you guys came down and got the school to provide him services."

> "We were lost. We had no idea what we were dealing with. . . . We thought we were just bad parents."

I vaguely remembered that Helen and I had gone to a meeting at the school about Brian, something we did routinely and that I continue to do for the kids I see today. Parents often say it's the most valuable single hour I spend on behalf of their child and family.

Charlene continued, "He had no conscience. He seemed unable to learn from his mistakes. He didn't have the ability to feel remorse for what he did. We tried another psychiatrist after we left you, but that doctor just dropped the ball. Brian was stealing from stores, stealing mail, lighting fires." That's when he was referred to Longview, an outpatient psychiatric school/facility for children who break the law. I waited with a bit of curious dread to hear what happened with Brian once he got to Longview.

"Brian continued to get into trouble. There was this program up in Sacramento, a children's home. Twenty-four-hour behavior modification. Only twelve kids in the entire program. They didn't use medications. But we couldn't afford to send Brian there."

I could tell that we were coming to a part of the story that was difficult for Charlene to relate, even thirty years later, and could understand why. The events and details struck at the core of her

"He had no conscience. . . . Brian was stealing from stores, stealing mail, lighting fires."

sense of responsibility and competency in her role as Brian's mother. How hard this is for all the mothers and fathers I meet over their children's problems, I thought.

She continued, "But if he had a criminal record and we made him a ward of the state, then the state would pay for him. So we pressed several charges against our own son. It was so hard, such a hard time." She paused. "But he was accepted to live up there. He actually lived up there for five years. He was the longest resident on record living there.

"By twelve or thirteen, his hyper-ness had calmed down but he still was making bad decisions," she continued. "He'd come home for a visit and things were still bad. But something happened around age sixteen. He started acting like a leader and mentor to the younger kids. By seventeen, he seemed much more mature. He came home to live with us at that point and he never was in trouble with the law again."

Amazing! I thought to myself. What a story. I was already glad I'd called. "What does Brian do now?"

"He's a long-distance truck driver. He drives mostly at night. He's still got little things. He forgets birthdays. He still doesn't think outside the box. He's not big on abstraction. But we paid his way through truck-driving school and he's wholly self-sufficient. We have good relations with him and speak to him regularly."

I asked them about their other son, Albert. "What about Albert? How is he doing?"

"Al is a successful real estate broker in Mill Valley [an affluent suburb of San Francisco]," Charlene explained. "But he really doesn't have a very close relationship with his brother anymore. That's too bad, but understandable, considering how different they are." Charlene sounded a little sad.

I pressed for a few more details. "What about Brian's social relationships? Has he been married? Does he have a steady girlfriend?"

"He really hasn't had satisfying relationships." Again, she sounded a bit wistful. "With women, he's shown poor judgment. He has a high rate of sexual activity, but no long-term relationships and no children that we know about. He works nights. He likes to sleep." I wondered what she meant by "a high rate of sexual activity" but thought that, thirty years later, I could live with the ambiguity.

While some might view Brian's life as limited, I felt he'd had a "good enough" outcome. Despite his very, very rough start, he had a regular, well-paying job, was a taxpayer and not a felon, and had maintained a decent relationship with his parents. I told Charlene what I thought, and she agreed.

"He leads a normal life. We're satisfied with how things turned out. We felt so alone before coming to see you. You gave us some help and some hope. We're so glad that you called. I always wanted to thank you."

I didn't know how to respond. I was surprised and deeply moved by her gratitude, and grateful to have learned more about this boy, who was so pivotal in my education about Ritalin's effects on children.

"What's the name of the book Brian's in?" she asked me.

"*Running on Ritalin*," I told her. "I chose the name 'Brian Hanas' [which rhymes with his real surname] because it sounded like the word 'heinous'—I thought Brian was very hard."

"That's okay," Charlene said with a sigh. "He *was* very hard."

4

. . .

ADHD Girls Grow Up

In *Running on Ritalin*, Jenny Carter was a sweet, dreamy ten-year-old who just worked too slowly at school and at home. As I noted:

> One of thirty-three children in her class, she often had trouble fin-
> ishing her assignments and would have to miss recess to make up
> the work . . . but they didn't see any signs that she was hyperactive
> or impulsive at all. Nor was her conduct a problem at home or at
> school. In fact, she was well liked by her friends. . . . She did have
> a tendency to daydream and even seemed to move physically more
> slowly than other kids, as if her inner clock was set at a more lei-
> surely pace. It took her longer to get things done—even things she
> liked—and she was tardy in completing chores at home, though her
> parents felt they could handle that problem.

Despite some behavioral interventions, Jenny continued to struggle, and wound up taking Ritalin for at least two years. My narrative

on Jenny ends at that point, and for this book, I hoped to learn how she was doing in her mid-twenties. My expectation, based on her solid "emotional intelligence"—her ability to sensitively read and respond to others' social cues—was that Jenny would be doing well, perhaps working at a job that involved interacting with people: sales, child care, or elder care, for example.

The point I was trying to make in telling the "Jenny story" in my earlier book was that here was a child who was pretty wonderful in many ways but was taking Ritalin to help her get through school because she had some learning and processing problems. Though she was "dreamy" and more internally distracted, she was neither hyperactive nor disruptive.

I was convinced that "my" Jenny and the hundreds of children like her whom I've seen over the years have happier, more productive lives once they're out of school. Their skills in dealing with people can lead to the more satisfying adult relationships that in large studies (and in my own small cohort of young adults as well) are more commonly consistent with self-described happiness and contentment than are academic or career achievement.

After searching through my records and notes and being frustrated in my attempts to identify her, I concluded that Jenny may have been a clinical composite of several girls I knew at that time. So instead of Jenny, I selected two other girls with similar circumstances—Lauren and Jennifer—to interview. Lauren was ten and Jennifer was eleven when I worked with them in the mid-1990s, and both were twenty-six when I interviewed them for this book. As children, both women flirted with the ADHD diagnosis and Ritalin, but like so many of the children described in *Running on Ritalin*, their outcomes had less to do with ADHD and Ritalin and more to do with other aspects of their personalities and family situations.

VICTIMIZED BY LIFE

Lauren was in the fourth grade when I first met her in 1994. Her family had moved from Mississippi to the Bay Area the year before, when her father, who worked in a technical field, accepted a job here. Eighteen months earlier, she had been seen by a neurologist and psychologist; her parents said doctors felt Lauren was "borderline ADD and H"—inattentive but also hyperactive. Following are highlights from my notes.

From her parents: *She still has trouble focusing: we must repeat instructions four or five times when being told what to do. . . . She has social issues with friends: acts spontaneously, impulsive, low patience level. More trouble in larger groups. But she always has one good friend. . . . She tests very bright. . . . Her behavior is a problem in the classroom. . . . Now we are considering medication. . . . She's been somewhat withdrawn from kids recently.*

From Lauren, at first meeting: *"I'm supposed to be in 5th but I'm only in 4th. I have an 'ADD problem' [trouble paying attention]. I keep reading in class. My teacher will ask me a question. I won't be able to answer."*

Lauren seems a bit depressed or tired. Her play in the sand tray (a small sandbox with table legs) is somewhat sparse, needs encouragement but then, when she said she was finished, kept adding stuff to the tray. She is very strong in reading and comprehension. Very strong in math. Her written language is average. Shows no signs of inattention or distractibility.

From a meeting with Lauren and her family: *Lauren uncomfortable and passively resistant. Tom, her father, has higher expecta-*

tions and is tougher than Nancy, her mother. Tom is the leader and the rest follow. Nancy with possible depression (says she's better). Lauren comes in and out of the discussion as she pleases but can contribute a lot.

From her teacher: *Strong academically, adjustment in moving (from Mississippi), difficulty with peers (easily irritated, hurt, sensitive, can be impulsive); doesn't always get the work done; more oppositional.*

As with Jenny, I didn't believe Lauren had ADHD or ADD. I thought she was a bright, unhappy, somewhat angry child who was struggling socially. I tried to get the parents to be more consistent with her and to have her mother increase her expectations and follow through on those expectations. I also suggested that her father back off a bit on his criticism and spend some positive time with her. When after two months there were only slight changes, Lauren's parents asked me to prescribe medication.

Reluctantly, I agreed, and put Lauren on Ritalin (5 to 15 milligrams once a day, in the morning); I also asked her teacher and parents to keep a daily log of her behavior. After two weeks on this regimen, I saw Lauren again; according to my notes, she had "minimal response to medication. The 'wall' is up. A sad and angry kid who keeps things to herself." I had only one more visit with Lauren and her family; her father appeared more appreciative of his daughter's strengths, but her mother continued to have problems setting and maintaining limits.

The last entry in my notes on Lauren concerned a phone call I had with her father in October 1994: "Things are going much better. Better at school. Some irrationality (teenage stuff). Likes boys. Maybe get her a horse. She's getting things done. Her mother is showing more responsibility."

I found Lauren via her sister, who had a page on Facebook. (I had tried Lauren's name and received too many matches.) Her sister gave me Lauren's phone number and told me to call her, which I did. I can't imagine what it was like for Lauren to receive a call from a doctor she had seen when she was a child. Understandably, she was hesitant at first. I gave her a brief description of our encounters years earlier, and she vaguely remembered. I told her about *Running on Ritalin* and my current project, and suggested that she check out my website. Following two or three exchanges over a two-week period, Lauren agreed to meet with me.

When she came to my office, I didn't recognize her. Lauren was a big woman, somewhat overweight, with residual acne. It seemed to be difficult for her to smile. I asked her what she recalled from our earlier sessions. "I remember feeling constantly berated by my teachers for not paying attention in class. [In my former school] we had already learned a great deal of what they were teaching me in California. It was boring. I'd draw in my notebooks instead of doing what they wanted me to do. The teachers would call up my parents. 'She needs to see someone,' they would say. I was already done with my work and then I'd do what I liked. I liked Mrs. R. [the teacher quoted in my notes]. It was another teacher that I had problems with.

> "I remember feeling constantly berated by my teachers for not paying attention in class. . . . They wanted to fix things by changing me."

"I doodled. I had a notebook filled with pictures of horses. I was also having a hard time making friends, so I chose to read. It was safe and made it easier to ignore people. My performance at school was the main issue. But they [her parents] were also concerned that I didn't have friends. I was the new girl. The other kids already knew one another. I didn't understand why nobody was listening to me."

Once she got started, the story poured out. The memories seemed fresh, and still painful. She displayed a sense of persecution—a belief that people didn't understand or were against her—that was similar to the theme I noticed when she was eleven.

"They wanted to fix things by changing me. I didn't think I was doing anything that bad. I scored high on IQ tests and they couldn't understand why I was still acting foolish in class. 'Because you're smart, you should know.' My mom made me take a test for gifted kids. It was a special class and I remember that I purposefully failed the test. I kept trying to meet their standards and they kept on raising them. It seemed like nothing pleased them. So I figured out if I did lousy, they would expect less and I wouldn't be picked on."

I asked her about her mother. "Mom would drive me to horse-back riding [lessons] and we'd also go shopping. I have some good memories." I think she was aware of how negative and pained she sounded and wanted me to know it hadn't all been bad.

When I inquired about her experience with Ritalin, she said it tasted bad. Ritalin is supposed to be swallowed, not chewed, but she said the pill sometimes dissolved in her mouth and made her slightly sick. "I never really felt right when I'd take the pills. It made me seem weird. The kids at school found out and teased me. I think the teacher may have mentioned it in class, and that's all they needed to hear."

We then moved on to her middle school years. "When I started middle school, I saw a female psychologist. I was depressed. The kids were vicious and mean. I was overall doing well in my classes. At the psychologist's office, I would sit and talk and she would take notes. I was trying to explain my point of view about trying to be nice to the other kids, but that they were mean, and the only thing I could do is be mean back. I'd get physical. This girl Jessica was out to get me." The tone of her voice revealed the hurt and passion she still felt about these long-ago incidents. At this point, I felt certain she was also emotionally struggling in the present.

"I would hide around corners. I would run from her. She pinched me under my arms one time and then I slammed her against the wall—'Don't fuckin' touch me!' I said. She got suspended. I didn't. My dad finally got involved. 'I'll sue the school,' he said. He called her parents and said they could duke it out.

"I was big, overweight, developed, with braces." In the margin of the paper on which I was taking notes, I jotted, "Whew! Her pain is still there." I tried to move her past this by asking about her high school experiences, which she said were better. "The people were less focused on image. They grew up. I actually made friends in high school. We were the social outcasts. We weren't Goths—we were the gamers.

"I did pretty good in high school academically. I met my friend Meredith and we became good friends. But there was a lot of drama surrounding her. Like she was trying to stay away from another friend who hated me. Her boyfriend was also drama. I kept on thinking, 'Why do these people hate me?' They conspired to try to embarrass me."

Again, I considered how this young woman suffered and was likely still suffering from some form of social isolation. The hurt appeared as fresh as though the events had happened just yesterday. At twenty-six, she could still recall these real (and some most likely imagined) slights.

She went on to describe her post–high school years. "I wanted to be a vet. I went to Humboldt [a state college in the extreme north of California]. I wanted to get away from the drama of high school, to get away from Meredith. So I chose the farthest school in the state. I did it for a year. I was lonely there, too. I thought maybe I should major in computer science. It wasn't easy, though; I nearly flunked. Then I went to a community college for two years, and was able to transfer to Sacramento State. But I just couldn't handle computer science. I almost flunked again. At that point, I changed to criminal justice. I took classes at night, and they were much easier. I watched the cop shows so I knew stuff. I liked it. It took four years for me to graduate; I commuted the last semester from my parents' house. It was a long drive. It was lousy."

Further discussion revealed that she had graduated the month before our interview; I was surprised—at almost twenty-seven, she had just earned an undergraduate degree. She was a bright enough kid, so that wasn't her problem. I asked about her plans for the future and she said she was looking at a career in law enforcement, possibly combining it with computer science. At the moment, however, she was working in sales at a local electronics store and living with her parents. "I don't have to pay rent. I've got low expenses so I can pay off my credit card debt. I'm able to go to the gym and maybe lose some pounds so I can qualify for the military."

Once our conversation moved into relationships, her sense of betrayal and victimhood surfaced again. "I've had only a few longer-lasting relationships, but somehow if I don't become useful to people, I'm put off to the wayside. Like they say, 'I'm friends with Lauren because I feel sorry for her.' I had a sort of boyfriend. I met him online. He was from Australia. I went to see him, and he saw me but then he cheated on me with one of my friends. That was four years ago and I'm over it some now." But I saw her color change. She wasn't over it.

"I met Terry online, too. It got weird—all online. Her husband was acting dangerous. She was up north, in Portland. She came down and lived with me for six months. She was also sick with Lyme disease." She told me that the relationship with Terry ended when she had to give up her apartment. "My parents thought Terry was leeching from me. But I still talk to her. I want my own place again. She'd be invited. It was the best time when she was living with me." I wondered if they shared more than a friendship—were they intimate? After our meeting, I wondered whether sexual identity issues contributed to part of Lauren's general unhappiness.

She paused and was silent. I waited a moment, and then asked what she was thinking. It was about Meredith. "I trusted her. It was a big blowup. It was complicated. There was a guy. I may have loved him—*but not too seriously*. He suddenly ditched me. I wanted Meredith to be supportive, but she said it was my fault.

"When the guy dropped me, I was a wreck. I called the suicide hotline. There was nobody around that weekend. I saw a psychologist intern at the school. I had ten free sessions and felt better. I tried a mild dose of Prozac. It mellowed me out. I used it for three months. But it was too expensive and I didn't need it."

We talked a bit about her immediate family. Her sister was a teacher in Oakland, California, and her younger brother was in college studying engineering. "I talk to them, but we're not especially close."

"What about your parents? How's your relationship with them?" I asked.

"My dad is the more difficult of the two. I try to be passive and let him have his rage fits and he'll back away. I learned that being too defensive doesn't work, so I pretend to go along with him; I'm the more easygoing one. I can talk to my mom, but I don't like to stress her out. She was really depressed. She had cervical cancer." Lauren looks sad again as she continues, "She was never hospitalized for her depression but I'm protective of her. Dad can be antagonistic and mean."

"What I've gone through—the disappointments, the betrayals—has made me a bit jaded."

As we finished our conversation, I asked her to sum up for me what she learned or gained from all these experiences.

"What I've gone through—the disappointments, the betrayals—has made me a bit jaded. But I find my friends want to talk to me about their relationships. They appreciate my point of view—that it's better to be realistic and not too romantic."

DOES PERSONALITY CHANGE WITH TIME?

As I reread my fifteen-year-old notes and reviewed the interview, many thoughts crossed my mind. First, I felt sad. In meeting these young adults, I saw the major themes of their present lives, both good and bad, as streams flowing from their pasts. When the streams were rough, I wondered how I could have made a difference. I wondered what proportion of those negative streams was inherent, genetic, biochemical, and what proportion came from the environment—from their early experiences with family, teachers, and peers—or could have been influenced with treatment.

I will wait until Chapter 7 to fully explore the continuing nature-nurture dilemma, and especially whether interventions of any type, drug or nondrug, make a difference. Clearly, Ritalin wasn't for Lauren, but—with the failure of parenting and behavioral strategies—the parents' desire to use the medication with their daughter influenced my decision to give it a try.

Lauren's problems, once I met her, didn't strike me as fitting a textbook ADHD/ADD profile. However, her presentation as a potential ADD candidate (she wasn't especially hyperactive) was becoming typical by the early to mid-1990s and now is common. Teachers and parents consider virtually every form of childhood underperformance and misbehavior as possible ADHD/ADD. The doctor-led, drug-company-supported education of society has been quite successful—too successful, in my opinion.

By the late 1990s, following a trend I've mentioned that started first with parents and teachers, teenagers were describing their problems in school as lack of focus or concentration. Recently, a child of six repeated this explanation, no doubt having heard it often from the adults of his world.

Many of these children do have real problems with attention, impulsivity, and distractibility. Remember, I do believe ADHD/ADD exists. But doctors and psychologists are supposed to rule out other causes of these behaviors before assigning an ADHD diagnosis. Real-world practice and pragmatism, however, often lead to just the opposite. Once symptoms of a myriad of childhood problems—from learning issues to physical and emotional abuse—become categorized as signs of ADHD/ADD, medication is prescribed.

For example, stereotypically, girls do not act out as much under stress as boys do. They try to please. As with Jenny, when a learning or processing issue exists, they daydream, drift, act distracted, and are distractible. Outside of academic demands, this form of coping at home or with friends usually does not represent a serious symptom of impairment. However, in the academic environment, performance is critical to most parents, children, and their teachers, and all are quite aware of its importance.

The learning problem may or not may be identified. Many children are referred to me absent even the most cursory assessment of their learning abilities by a school psychologist or special education teacher. Many, many doctors, especially pediatricians, who write most of the country's Ritalin prescriptions, rely on symptom checklists filled out by one or both parents and the teacher to confirm an ADHD diagnosis. Then they say, "Why don't we try some Ritalin and see if it works?"

Many parents—not to mention doctors—still adhere to the notion that if Ritalin, a stimulant, "calms" the hyperactive child or improves school performance, it "proves" the kid has ADHD. In fact, Ritalin and all the other stimulants improve concentration for *everyone*, not just those with ADHD.

Indeed, Ritalin will often improve behavior and performance problems stemming from a host of causes (especially learning and processing problems). I've heard many general pediatricians and family doctors say (in part because of time and practice constraints), "Then why not use it?" The simple answer is, as mentioned previously, that a pill is not the moral equivalent to engagement with affected children.

After talking to Lauren, I wondered if extended individual or family psychotherapy could have helped her when she was younger, though her parents weren't interested in such a course at the time. Like hundreds of other unhappy children whom I've seen over the years, Lauren was brought to me for diagnosis and treatment of ADHD, but that diagnosis was not the best descriptor of her or the other children's problems. A thorough look at the entire child and his or her environment should be part of any evaluation and treatment. I am left feeling that perhaps I should have pursued this family more. Perhaps then I could have made more of a difference to Lauren. I will never know, but the thought haunts me.

ANOTHER ADHD CANDIDATE WITH A BETTER OUTCOME

Jennifer also initially came to me for an ADHD evaluation. As we will see, she, like Lauren, really did not meet my criteria for the diagnosis, but her outcome at age twenty-six is quite different from Lauren's. Since she had been in preschool, Jennifer's parents had thought there was "something different" about her. By the time she was in the fifth grade, she was described by both her previous and current teachers as having a hard time focusing. According to her parents, the school psychologist—after spending only ten minutes observing Jennifer in her classroom—decided she had ADD. Based on a questionnaire her parents filled out, a second doctor confirmed the ADD diagnosis and suggested medication, which her parents declined. (Her father, who said he had no patience, decided after reading the bestselling book *Driven to Distraction* that he, too, probably had adult ADD.)

I met Jennifer and her family a total of five times in the summer of 1996. Three of those times were devoted to taking a history and the assessment. During the fourth, I presented my findings to her parents and offered suggestions to help her. At the last visit, according to my notes, I gave her parents more specific approaches on parenting and school strategies for Jennifer, followed by a brief written report.

Here are some excerpts from my report on Jennifer:

Jennifer would score in the normal range of intelligence on formal psychometric testing. She demonstrated some mild visual errors in her reading and occasional auditory processing inconsistencies. However, none of these weaknesses constitutes a true learning disability. She displayed adequate reading and language arts skills. While she had a good grasp of math concepts, some of her math facts remain weak.

In this setting, she acted uncertain and less willing to take risks, which appeared reflective of some insecurity.

By history, both at home and at school, she has had some trouble with attention, distractibility, and task completion. Within the office setting, she had no trouble with attention, tended towards perfectionism, and if anything was too methodical, to the point of performing too slowly. Jennifer's behavior weakly meets criteria of either an attention deficit disorder (inattentive type) or over-

anxious disorder, or both. It is likely both attention and anxiety play roles in her underperformance, especially at school but also at home.

She has a history of trouble with longer-lasting peer relationships, which may be a reflection of her sensitivity and her difficulty responding to social cues. She is a bit bossy with her friends.

Jennifer's family is positive and caring. The parents appear caught between wanting to provide a supportive, protective environment for Jennifer while expecting a certain level of performance from her.

I think I must have sensed that the parents were simultaneously mixing nurturance with limit setting, which has a tendency to diminish the effectiveness of both. Her mother tended to be the nurturer and her father the limit setter. I had hoped that, between them, they could settle somewhere in the middle and be more consistent.

I suggested that they establish clear and immediate consequences (good and bad) for specific tasks. I told her mother to set aside time during the day to attend to Jennifer's complaints sympathetically, but otherwise to limit her response to them. I thought that spending positive time with her father might be the best reward for Jennifer. Longer-term counseling was suggested if brief interventions were not successful.

I also recommended that her teachers use a similar style of immediate rewards or consequences for specific tasks at school, and thought that individual private tutoring would be helpful as an emotional support rather than necessary for educational advancement. A structured or adult-supervised peer group activity was recommended to assist Jennifer in fostering better peer relationships.

The report concluded: "If other interventions are not successful, a trial of stimulant medication may be warranted several weeks into the new school year [I had seen them over the summer]. Introduction of any medication must be presented carefully to Jennifer because of her susceptibility to interpret such an intervention negatively upon her self-image." I said I would give them a call in a month to follow up; though I later left a message, I never heard back from them.

· · ·

It was relatively easy to track down Jennifer. Her mother remembered me and told me that Jennifer was living and working in Fresno; she also gave me her telephone number and email address. When we connected, Jennifer was quite willing to meet and be interviewed, and we set up a time for her to come to my office. When she arrived, I completely failed to recognize her. A bit on the stout side, she smiled widely and seemed comfortable from the start. As she walked through the office's three rooms, I asked what she remembered from our meetings when she was a child.

"I don't remember the waiting room. I thought there were only two rooms. I remember this low table. There was this big piece of paper and we all had to draw without talking. I even remember what I did. I did a face and my father added some ears, and I was very unhappy with his addition." Her memory of this family activity (which I've employed in assessments for more than thirty years) was acute and accurate. But I wasn't surprised. While children do not often remember conversation or content, they invariably recall playing with the toys and games or participating in an activity. Their parents are generally only slightly better at recalling the specifics of therapy sessions years earlier. Jennifer vaguely remembered the sandbox with the small toys, but had no memory of a scene she had created for me there.

We went over my brief report and I shared my feeling that, as a child, she was a perfectionist as well as anxious—demonstrated, for example, by the number of erasures she had just in copying some designs. She agreed that she really wanted to get things right, and that she was a pleaser. I told her that teachers had noted that her friendships were somewhat limited because if the kids didn't want to play her way, she wouldn't play at all. Jennifer also agreed with that, and that she was bossy, but said some of the "popular girls" who were more "girly" gave her a hard time in the fifth grade. She also concurred with my observation that her father tended to be more critical and her mother more worried. Though so much time had passed, I recognized her personality within the first fifteen minutes we spent together.

"I'm still intense," she said. "I look back at those times when I saw you. I had gone to really tough schools academically; two had accelerated programs." She recalled her fifth-grade teacher as especially inflexible, and admitted she had never liked her.

"I hated getting into trouble—I was very much a pleaser—but I remember Mrs. B-W saying (and I still hate it to this day), 'You have to . . .' and thinking to myself, 'Oh really?' Overall, I wanted others to get what they need. So I'd care too much. Some of that is still true today. In college, I wanted my professors to grade my tests right away so I could get immediate reactions. This is what I thrive on." I also thought to myself that, then and now, she had a streak of rebellion—she cared but she wasn't going to let anyone (even a teacher) boss her around. What I call persistence is often labeled as stubbornness in childhood and determination in the adult world.

"I agree with the things you picked up [power, intensity, sensitivity, anxiety]. To this day, I get into trouble with my boyfriend, who says 'Why do you care so much?' During middle school, I switched my group of friends. I was so tired of trying to please others that I gravitated to the Goth girls, who didn't seem to care what people thought. They were more carefree and didn't judge me. I remember I painted my fingernails alternately black and white. But at the end of seventh grade, my long-term friend, also named Jen-

"I remember I painted my fingernails alternately black and white."

nifer (she had been my friend since we were both two years old), said to me, 'Why are you hanging out with that group?' She reached out to me and I returned to my original set of friends.

"I fell in love with math in the eighth grade—it was algebra and I loved it. There was a certainty and logic to math. There were steps to take that were right." Her reasons for loving algebra made me think of her anxiety, perfectionism, and desire to please that may have hampered her performance in elementary and middle school. That, rather than distractibility or inattention, was her main problem. No wonder she gravitated toward the certainty and predictability of math.

"Over time, I figured out ways to work the system. When I went to high school, it wasn't as hard as the earlier grades. At one point I thought, 'Third grade was way harder.' I graduated high school with a 4.2 GPA. I learned how to work the AP physics teacher," she said both wryly and proudly. "But I didn't want to apply to the university system because I thought I might not get in. I knew I was a shoo-in for the state colleges and I preferred to be a big fish in a smaller pond. I went to Fresno State and it was cake. I got studying down to a science. But I still had this perfectionist side. I knew everything about the school, like when the books would become available for sale. I almost became an academic counselor, which led to my thinking that I might want to be some sort of counselor for work.

"I was a political science major, but the courses drove me crazy because there was all this talk without any answers (compared to math—I like structure and clarity). Then I decided to get a master's degree. I stayed at Fresno and got my MA in rehabilitative counseling. I just graduated in June."

Jennifer now works as a counselor with the State of California's

Department of Rehabilitation. It seems to suit her; as she noted, she loves talking to people and getting their stories.

She told me with a wink how she got her job, which was another example of her working the system. "I had to do an internship and I did it with the state agency in Fresno. They loved me in the internship. They didn't want to let me go, but they said they couldn't offer me a full-time job because of the cutbacks.

"My supervisor knew me from my master's program. She was from the same program. She told me about a job opening in Reno. I went up there and loved it. They offered me the job. I asked them for a bit of time to think it over. Fresno found out and then they offered me a full-time job and I took it.

> "There's a doctorate somewhere out there for me, but you have to pick your passions."

"I'm really happy but there's something still that says I could be doing more. There's a doctorate somewhere out there for me, but you have to pick your passions. I'd love to teach."

As though anticipating what I was thinking, she reflected on her personality. Did she think there was any ADD in her? "I'm still hard on myself. I don't give myself credit. I've still got a random [impulsive/tangential] side to me. For example, everyone could be talking about something important and I'll say, 'Oh, look at the elephant!' In fact, my nickname on my flag college team was 'Random.' I can see my train of thought, but unless I explain it to people, they don't get it. I have moments of impulsivity but I've learned how to rein it in [in] public situations."

Our conversation shifted to her social life and her relationship with boys. "I wasn't interested in boys until college. In my fantasy games when I was a little girl, I always played the older one. I was also the determined one. I would only play what I wanted to play. You know, I still have to learn how to be more accommodating. I have a stronger sense of self-awareness, partly through my studies. I can now adjust more easily; I do self-talk and it calms me down.

"Though I had two serious crushes in high school, I didn't have a boyfriend until I was nineteen. I was too busy with a half-dozen activities and AP classes; even now I have a very full day. I used to pick nerdy guys. Initially, they were assholes. I'd be with them just for the attention but I got over that fast. I met Greg six months ago at my best friend's wedding. He's in Los Angeles [about a three-hour drive from Fresno]. He works in visual effects." She told me they were seriously committed, for the moment.

Though her job paid rather poorly, it helped that she lived rent-free in a house her parents bought for her. She was also involved with many young adult activities sponsored by the local Catholic church. I asked about her current relationship with her parents, which she said was good, though her father still had the capacity to infuriate her. "I get explosive with him. That's because we're like each other. We're both hardheaded. My mom and I are more best friends than mother and daughter."

I also asked about her brother, who is two years younger than she is. "He's finishing at Sac State. He and my dad don't talk at all these days. Dad really pushed baseball on him. They broke with one another so that my brother could have a life. He doesn't have a clue, and it frustrates me. He's twenty-two! He's really the smarter kid but he's taken the easier route."

Jennifer, by far the most mature of the former patients I had talked to up to that point, remains intense, energetic, and lively, but far more positive than when she was a child and her insecurities were greater. She agreed she would have felt very bad about herself if she had taken medication.

Jennifer's mother was waiting for us after the interview. She greeted me warmly and was eager to share an incident that just occurred as she ate lunch near Kaiser Hospital. "I brought your book

[*Running on Ritalin*] with me to read during lunch. Well, while I was reading it, a nurse came up to me and said, 'You know, that's a very good book.'" I was quite tickled. The three of us shook hands and said our good-byes.

· · ·

Two girls, both preteens when I met them, with similar streaks of intensity and determination, seem so different thirteen years later. Why? What was it about who they were and what had happened to them that could lead to such different outcomes? Both were referred to me to consider or rule out ADHD. Upon reflection, I could see there were elements in their personalities that may have contributed to moments of impulsive and distractible behavior, but these features certainly weren't central to their problems back then. I'm glad I recognized at the time the secondary nature of their ADHD symptoms. Their outcomes seem to vindicate that judgment.

I can only guess at the reasons for their differences. Somehow, Lauren's sense of victimhood, seeing herself as suffering unjustly as a result of the actions of others, limited her and likely led to over-reaction and self-fulfilling negative outcomes.

Jennifer was also "in trouble" as a young girl, but somehow, her experiences translated into a model of being able to work the system. Did she just have a sunnier disposition than Lauren? Is disposition innate, or can it be learned? I suspect it's mostly the former, but early experiences in life are also important. I'm left with feeling that, as the doctor, I'm only an observer to life's unfolding more often than I care to admit.

5

. . .

Living with ADHD
Finding the Right Job

While Evan was not a patient I featured in *Running on Ritalin*, I believe that his story is quite revealing about the course of ADHD, and therefore should be told here. Of all my patients, he has also taken Ritalin the longest; now twenty-four, he has been on the drug (or some variation) continuously since 1997.

I first met Evan in May 1994 when he was finishing third grade at a local private Christian school. Here are some of my verbatim chart notes:

> *Trouble bringing stuff home, "Oh, I forgot it." Mom has to tell him [to do his homework] repeatedly. Mom has to be right there for homework. As, Bs, Cs at school. Auditory processing problem noted; six years old in first grade. Sits in the front of the room in school. Minimal distractions there. Not hyper. Still reverses words and letters. In his first visit with his parents and brother, Evan sits*

quietly and is attentive, but can become distracted the moment the
conversation involves someone else. Alone, Evan was attentive,
thoughtful, and worried about his father's health. [His father had
multiple health problems: bad back, kidney issues, and depression.]
On educational screening, problems with auditory processing
(remembering sequential commands) and weaker in reading com-
prehension. Some distractibility noted but not in one-on-one situ-
ations.

Evan's mother, who seemed to operate as the "frontal lobe/
executive function" of the family's "brain," was quite exasperated
with both her husband and her sons. In addition to his health problems, Evan's father thought he might have ADD. (This was two
years before the publication of *Driven to Distraction*.)

My evaluation led me to believe that Evan's problems were
more likely to be educational and developmental than ADD-
related. For example, auditory processing weakness—which often
presents as trouble following the teacher's instructions—is one of
the biggest mimickers of ADD. In both cases, the child doesn't follow through, is confused, and appears to daydream, or wanders to
another classroom "distraction."

Initial interventions for learning and developmental problems
are quite similar to the nondrug interventions for ADD; indeed,
when these prove insufficient, the universal performance-enhancing
effects of Ritalin are appropriate additives to the mix. I suggested
to Evan's parents that they continue with educational support, offer
immediate reinforcers (tangible rewards and consequences) for
completing tasks on time at school and at home, and undergo a
couple of counseling sessions in order to learn to work more effectively as a team. I also referred them to a learning specialist whom
I deeply respect for her ability to teach reading to even the most

learning-disabled children. Later that year, I noted in my files that her report essentially cleared Evan of any serious learning disabilities and ADD, even though she noted the reports of distractibility in the classroom setting. Her educational recommendations were similar to mine.

TIME FOR RITALIN

After this, it was two and a half years before I saw Evan and his parents again; at that point, Evan was one month into seventh grade. As I noted in his record, "He's getting fair grades but losing out because of late or failed assignments. He is still going off for the wrench and winds up spending time on something else." The "wrench" reference was shorthand for the almost obsessive interest Evan demonstrated in cars and auto mechanics. His father taught vocational car repair at the local high school, and the family had several vehicles in various states of completion on their property, which made his fascination even easier to indulge.

A call to one of his teachers confirmed both the missed assignments and ongoing distractibility in the classroom. A week later, I began prescribing Ritalin to Evan, ultimately 20 milligrams three times a day. In fact, for quite some time after the introduction of the long-acting methylphenidate products such as Concerta, Evan still followed his three-times-a-day Ritalin regimen. This preference for an established routine—and active avoidance of change—was a prominent feature of Evan's personality, both then and now.

Evan performed adequately in high school and was deeply involved in his father's car repair classes, going so far as to assist him in teaching on occasion. Therefore, it was not a great surprise when, in his senior year, Evan told me he wasn't planning to go to college.

He and his parents had found a full-time vocational car repair program in Phoenix, Arizona, and he had enrolled in it.

I referred Evan to a doctor I knew in Phoenix, who helped him manage his medication during the eighteen months he lived there. When he returned to the Bay Area in 2005, we resumed our therapeutic relationship; I have seen him every six months since for a "check-in" on his life and medication. At the time, he was still taking Ritalin, but had cut his dose to twice a day. In 2006, I finally convinced Evan to switch to the more convenient once-a-day Concerta, which he takes six days a week.

Evan has lived with his parents since he returned from Arizona, but could easily live on his own. After completing a BMW certified technician's program, he was immediately hired by a local BMW dealer as one of their repairmen. He estimates his annual salary at $40,000; some of his fellow techs, with many more years of experience, are earning close to six figures.

On the day of our interview, for which he took time off from work, Evan told me he had not taken his morning Concerta dose. Evan is stocky to overweight, and prematurely balding. He speaks in a steady and forthright manner, and there was nothing very "hyper" about him, nor had there ever been.

I began the interview by asking him to tell me about his earliest memories of coming to my office, which began when he was in the third grade. His recollections from those early years were fuzzy; about the only thing he could recall were the sand tray and its toys, and making drawings. "I remember it as mostly boring," he said.

"I was still at an evangelical private school—that's when I start remembering you . . . in the seventh grade. I had an attitude. I felt like the school day was my workday, and then homework was just too

"There was lots of yelling [by his parents]: 'Get your work done. You're grounded!'"

much. I just didn't do my homework. I'll work on cars all day, but then after, I'll do my own thing. That was my attitude in high school, also. So there was lots of yelling [by his parents]: 'Get your work done. You're grounded!'"

Of his relationship with Ritalin, he commented that he knew it was supposed to help him focus. "Without it, I'd disappear into my own little world—daydreaming—and the distractions would get me. It didn't bother me to take it. 'It won't make you do the work,' you said, 'but it'll help you if you want to do it.'" I say the same thing to my current patients, and was surprised that he was able to quote me so precisely.

"I had to go to the office for the second pill of the day. I didn't care. It didn't bother me. It really never came up with the other kids. All my friends knew, but they didn't care about my 'meds.' There was nothing really bad about taking them. Only if I took it late, then I couldn't sleep. It was weird not to be hungry, but I'd just eat later. In high school, I took the second dose in my dad's class-room. I was in there during my free time most of the time anyway."

I asked him why he stayed with the two- to three-times-a-day dose of Ritalin when he could have taken once-a-day Concerta.

"I resisted trying Concerta because the Ritalin had been work-ing. It [the multiple doses] did finally become a hassle, so I switched to Concerta. I'm a creature of habit. Little distractions still bother me. I could still sit and work on my snowmobile [without the med-ication], for example, but it would take me way longer to do it. With-out the med, I have to really buckle down. I have to concentrate to concentrate. It's definitely harder." I asked him if he felt there were any downsides to taking the medicine now. "Only if I take it late, like around noon or one. Then it keeps me up until midnight."

"Tell me how you wound up doing what you're doing now," I asked.

EVAN FINDS HIS NICHE

"I knew I wanted to do the automotive program as early as sixth or seventh grade. With the vocational track, I found there were things I didn't have to take—I didn't have to take a language. I was too detailed. I have horrible amounts of perfectionism. Just one thing out of place and . . . The medicine helps me prioritize just a little bit."

I had always suspected that Evan had a streak of perfectionism but had never before heard him articulate it so clearly. It was the perfectionism that made him anxious and led to his tendency to operate meticulously and slowly—that is, not getting tasks done at school in "a timely fashion." This "comorbidity" added to what I had always considered his rather mild case of ADD. The benefit of the medication was that it helped him work more efficiently, which satisfied both his innate perfectionist streak and also addressed his ADD tendencies.

We then moved on to a discussion of Evan's social life.

"I didn't have too many friends in middle school—I found my group in high school. We're still friends today. I went go-carting last week with some of them, and this winter, we'll go snowmobiling." When I asked him if he dated, he looked a little chagrined, and embarrassed for the first time. "I'm very shy. I hope I'm not a confirmed bachelor. My parents, my friends—they try to hook me up with girls. My parents say, 'Get out,' and I say I'm happy at home with my 'toys.'" He has three cars, a snowmobile, and his video games. He seemed relieved when we started talking about his job.

"I've worked for BMW for four and a half years. I've worked my way up. Not too high, but I'm a master technician. I have all my certifications but I'm sure they'll come up with some new ones for me to have to get. [One of] my foremen has had it out for me since day one. He makes cutting remarks about me. He thinks he's better than me. My other foreman is fine, but this one blames me for everything. I intend to talk to my manager about him."

While it seemed to be a minor thing, Evan's point was that "the system" was generally out to shaft him. He had to be alert and stay on top of things; otherwise he would lose out. This attitude was reflected in his comments, which often displayed a darkly humored sense of injustice for the common guy—specifically, for himself.

Evan continued, "I'm still working on the used cars [preparing them for resale by the dealer]. I was in the service department for a year. Four of us work together as a team. I like to get there early. I get a good parking spot. I work up to twelve hours a day, but I'm not paid hourly, I'm paid by the job. I liked being team leader—we rotate. I'd get there even earlier and set out everything. I earn enough these days; it's not as much as I'd like, but my living expenses are minimal."

I thought to myself that Evan's horizons were very narrow. "How's living at home with your parents?" I asked.

"I got used to it. I want out, though. They want me out, too. I get along with them, but it's time for me to go. We own four homes on the street. We've done all the work ourselves on the houses, except the electrical stuff." The properties owned by Evan's family were actually quite valuable—a testimony to his parents' frugality and shrewd early home investments in the ultimately outrageously expensive Bay area.

Evan told me that his father's health had improved, and that his mother had lost both her parents but was doing better than he expected. His brother, whom I'd also treated, was working at the same BMW dealership; Evan had helped him get a job there. At first, he was washing cars, but had advanced to doing bodywork. After high school, his brother had attended the same school as Evan and was trained to repair computer hardware, but didn't want to make the commute a job in his field would require (whereas the dealership is only ten minutes from their house).

Then we got to the question I'd been waiting to ask. "How would you evaluate my role with you and your family through the years?"

"No one has had a problem with you. You've been helpful, but not in any way I can easily describe. You've helped the family relax some. We're not so high-strung. You know, you've 'got to be good for the doctor,' be on your best behavior. I think that's helped."

He went on to say that he'd like to lose some weight, and that his hair loss was really bothering him. I asked him if he'd thought about trying Rogaine, but he said he wasn't interested. He shaved his head instead, which, he said, "bugged the heck out of my mom."

THE ALL-IMPORTANT MOTIVATION FACTOR

More than ever, Evan struck me as a creature of habit. His father was the last vocational auto shop teacher in the school district, and like his dad, Evan loved cars. He'd been on this track since age twelve. Going away to technical school after high school instead of to community college was a great thing, both for his training and his emotional growth—it was one period of time in his life where Evan moved out of his comfort zone and was quite successful.

He seemed satisfied with what he has, despite his sense that society's powerful people have it out for the little guys (like him). He has a job where he may well remain for the next thirty years. I predict he'll find a girl—or rather, she'll find him. His mother is the family general and his father is fairly passive, much like Evan. And so it goes.

As I look back on my former patients, Evan serves to highlight a common trajectory for children with ADD/ADHD. Like all children, as they age and become more mature, they have an increasing number of choices about how they spend their time. For more than a century, education has been compulsory in the United States; in most states, children must attend school at least to the age of sixteen. Our government (and culture) decided long ago that an educated citizenry is critical to a well-functioning democracy. But school has become the child's essential job. As farming and even manufacturing employment have become less viable, a college education is seen

School has become the child's essential job.

as the best guarantee of economic success. And like it or not, society's focus on consumer spending and materialism means that making money has become equivalent to being happy. Thus, children learn at an early age that good school performance and higher education are mandatory.

The pressure on children to perform academically is enormous, and is shared by their families and teachers. I have no doubt that this pressure is one of the factors fueling the ADHD/Ritalin boom that began in the early 1990s and continues to this day. In the United States, education is highly language-oriented, and math and logic abilities are also valued.

Many other countries, such as Japan and Germany, beginning in high school, have multiple tracks that separate students who display a capacity for college-level work from those who are more suited to (or more interested in) technical or vocational training. Conversely, in the United States, Canada, and Australia, everyone hopes they can be a Steve Jobs and feels they should be allowed that right. Ironically, this puts more pressure on kids, families, and teachers. So it's no surprise that these three countries have some of the highest per capita rates of Ritalin use in children in the world. There are probably many reasons for this, including the cultural influence of the United States on other English-speaking countries. Still, Canada's rate is one-third that of the United States'. The United Kingdom has a rate of Ritalin use that, while growing, is less than one-tenth of ours. In comparison, Japan's use is an infinitesimal 1.4 percent of ours (see the postscript).

What if a child's talents lie in other realms? Since the 1980s, scientists have described "multiple intelligences," including athletic, artistic, and interactional, to name just a few. But notwithstanding the special education movement, the square educational hole that every child must fit into is increasingly inflexible, and Ritalin is often the lubricant for the round, triangular, or octagonal-shaped young mind.

I've already employed the metaphor of the child's sorting toy to describe the "friction," or poor fit, between a child's talents and the demands and responses of the environment that often lead to an ADHD diagnosis and the prescribing of Ritalin. When I talk to parents, I also use an equation to highlight the factors that contribute to a child's behavior or school problems: Performance = (Talent + Temperament) × Motivation. This equation is meant only to highlight the various factors of performance and is not intended to be psychometrically precise.

Performance = (Talent + Temperament) × Motivation

The Performance (including behavior) of the child at school is made up of three components that combine and influence one another. In this equation, Talent means the child's basic abilities, developmental and academic strengths and weaknesses. Learning disabilities or global delay—that is, an across-the-board learning weakness—results in a low Talent, whereas academically gifted children have a high Talent rating.

Temperament refers to the child's personality—those aspects of behavior that are felt as inherent and genetic to the child. Some children, by nature, are very persistent and very eager to please. Their Temperament factor is high. Others tend to give up easily or are more interested in pleasing themselves. Some children—whom we typically label ADHD—have trouble making a sustained effort and utilizing their knowledge of delayed consequences to make decisions in the present. We call that last quality "impulsivity." ADHD contributes to a low Temperament factor.

Most ADHD evaluations focus on children's Talents and Temperament. But Motivation is also a critical factor, particularly as children get older. Virtually all children make efforts to cooperate and learn in kindergarten and first grade. But I routinely see children who, even by second grade, are beginning to give up or make less-than-maximum effort to do their schoolwork in class or at home.

Even without a Talent or Temperament issue, Motivation declines for most children during the middle school years. Children with a high Talent factor or with good work habits survive this predictable decline in Motivation. But younger adolescents whose Talent or Temperament is shaky often experience a precipitous decline in Motivation, leading to big decreases in Performance from sixth grade to about age sixteen or seventeen. (As mentioned previously, Russell Barkley and I discussed this phenomenon in detail in the essay "Entering the Valley of Motivational Fatigue: ADHD in Early Adolescence," in *The Last Normal Child*.)

Essentially, Motivation is key and is influenced by success, or lack of it. But until mid to late high school, children generally have little choice in what they must learn or study, which would present a motivational challenge for most of us. Some go to schools that specialize in the arts or (rarely) a technical trade. It isn't until they're out of high school that children face, or are allowed, a choice in what they must do in their "job."

So many of the children I see who meet ADD criteria and take Ritalin are going through a temporary phase of decreased Motivation. In the post–high school years, they find their niche and no longer want or need the drug. Only two of the ten young adults I interviewed for this book currently use Ritalin regularly. Evan, whom I include to demonstrate an entirely different but successful path, is the only person who has taken it continuously from middle school days. I'll explain why in a moment.

Over and over, I've observed that by the time children are in their early to mid-twenties, they are finding a niche, a position, a vocation that works for them, one that matches up with their Talent and Temperament proclivities. Their Motivation increases as a result of their natural interests and because they are having success. Many try college because they've been told it's the optimal road to success, but it doesn't work for them, and they fail or drop out. But fortunately, in the larger working world, there are many jobs for which a four-year degree is either unnecessary or not helpful. I remind my teenage patients that some form of post–high school training is almost always required to get an adequately paying, self-supporting job, but it doesn't have to be college.

After reviewing my notes, I came to a new conclusion about Evan's continued Ritalin use. I never really saw him as having a major case of either ADHD or ADD, but his grades, which were mediocre without medication, improved somewhat when taking the drug. He told me many times that it was easier—and remains easier—to read and remember what he reads when he takes Ritalin. I do believe that he has minor dyslexia, which the Ritalin helps.

But in Evan's case, I've come to appreciate the importance of both his innate perfectionism and his inertia. When evaluating adults for ADHD, I am faced with trying to decide whether they experience true underperformance or have impossible-to-meet expectations of themselves. Sometimes the underperformance is obvious. But most of the time, I've been more impressed with the anxiety these adults have over what most would consider adequate or better-than-adequate performance. This seems to be the case with Evan. Also, all aspects of Evan's behavior are affected by his profound level of inertia. It took me seven years to convince him to try Concerta once he had become used to Ritalin. There's a strong

When evaluating adults for ADHD, I am faced with trying to decide whether they experience true underperformance or have impossible-to-meet expectations of themselves.

"let's not change anything if it's not badly broken" quality to everything Evan does, from his job to his personal life to his medication choices.

When I've asked Evan whether he thinks he still needs the drug, he's told me he doesn't feel as though he *needs* it, but that it makes it easier for him to read and stay organized at work. All right, then: Ritalin is everyman's performance enhancer. It appears to be a safe enough drug when used properly, and he believes it helps him. Consequently, I continue to prescribe it to him even though I don't think he has a serious case of adult ADHD.

Some readers may think my position hypocritical or even unethical. If I don't believe Evan has a major disorder, shouldn't I just stop prescribing him Ritalin? I actually believe long term (and I work long term) that Evan will eventually come to that conclusion himself. In the meantime, I believe Evan has achieved a great deal as a young adult, especially given his very rough start in the early grades. I think Ritalin played a significant role in his success, and if he feels it still is necessary, for the moment I can support his decision comfortably.

WHO WANTS TO BE A MILLIONAIRE?

Cameron was mentioned only briefly in *Running on Ritalin*. His father, Paul, was featured—an adult who struggled with alcohol and briefly abused Ritalin when I prescribed it to him. But I've included Cameron's story here because I think it beautifully illustrates the finding-your-niche challenge for the ADHD child and adult.

I met Cameron in 1991, when he was eight and in the second grade (he had repeated first grade). Here are some selected chart notes from my first encounter with his parents:

Parents' theory . . . ADD. Difficulty concentrating. Impulsive . . .
pounded on his sister. "Sometimes we're not sure that he fully 'gets'
it." He can play with his Ninja Turtles for long periods. Held back
for social-emotional reasons last year. Going to weekly group ther-
apy at school.

Notes upon meeting Cameron for the first time:

"Kids bug me, they scream in my ear." He squiggles on his chair
and moves it as we talk. "Ashley [a classmate], I'd like to kick her,
get her into trouble or hurt her. Is there a camera here?" He's con-
cerned that someone is watching him or taping what he says. "I
fight with my sister over TV. We both get into trouble but she knows
how to make tears." He's distracted while we talk and changes
the subject several times. Three wishes . . . (1) all the money in the
world, (2) kids to rule the world, (3) more wishes. I insist on some-
thing more specific . . . Parents have to do school again so they can
have detention and suspensions.

Whew! My final note from this session was "acts angry and needs to dominate." There was so much going on with Cameron. His parents, Paul and Jeri, had very different expectations and ways of dealing with him. On top of that, they had their own problems, especially Paul, whom I later spent many months counseling. He wound up being hospitalized twice for substance abuse (alcohol and prescription drugs) and depression. On the plus side, they clearly loved their son, remained employed—Paul owned his own business—and have stayed together throughout the years. Jeri wins multiple Purple Hearts in my estimation, and I was also very fond of Paul, despite his erratic behavior.

Schoolwork wasn't easy for Cameron, though if he persevered, he could do it. His impulsivity and distractibility made the decision to prescribe Ritalin relatively clear-cut, and his parents committed to a long haul of family therapy, sustaining the effort for almost eight years, on and off. I started Cameron on a three-times-daily dose of Ritalin; later, because he didn't like taking the noontime dose at school, I switched him to Ritalin SR ("sustained release," though the SR version of Ritalin was never proven to last much longer than the standard tablet). Within two years, he required an additional midafternoon dose.

He remained on that regimen for more than five years. In December 1999, after several incidents in high school (writing a bad check, being arrested for vandalism, fighting, and driving his father's truck off the road), we tried Dexedrine Spansules and, finally, Concerta. The last time I saw Cameron was in June 2001, and I wrote my final prescription for him that September. A year later, I received a photocopied Christmas letter from Jeri. In it, she wrote that Cameron "is enrolled in the local college and does whatever it takes. Of course, his motivation is somewhere along the lines of 'he who finishes first—parties first.'" At the bottom of the letter, she added a handwritten note: "Glad we haven't needed you recently. Kinda miss 'your mug' though."

That was my last contact with the family until I began setting up the interviews for this book and phoned Jeri to ask for Cameron's number. She was her warm and wisecracking self. Her humor kept her—as well as her family and even me at times—sane throughout the hard times. She thought Cameron would have no problem speaking with me and put me in touch with him.

When Cameron came into my office, I recognized him right away: square-jawed, solid, with the build of a middle linebacker. He was living in Pacifica, a beach community just south of San Francisco, and working for a caterer. He and his girlfriend, Nicole, a baker and chef, chose Pacifica because it's right on the water and has an active surfing community. They selected the house they were living in because it had a garage, which Cameron uses as a workshop in which he makes surfboards. His boards, known as "wave guns," are made for riding big waves. He told me he intends to surf Mavericks, an area internationally known for its annual big wave competition. He went on to say that he had several jobs but most of his income came from working for the caterer and selling Nicole's baked goods.

Cameron talked about his father's business. Paul was an independent mortician and had always railed against large corporate mortuaries. "He's getting by and hasn't sold out," Cameron said. When we moved on to a discussion of his school days, he recalled that his junior year was pretty rocky, both academically and behaviorally. "I spent my senior year at an alternative high school, which featured skiing at Lake Tahoe. I graduated but didn't get to participate in my high school graduation ceremonies." After high school, he took classes at a community college and was within a couple of credits of earning an AA degree in business.

"I've been trying to get a job as a firefighter for the last six years, interviewing up and down the state and taking the exams. I've scored high and have had three interviews. The average time it takes to get a firefighting job is seven to ten years, so I feel I'm still in the running. It's America's sexiest job. I want to be a 'hotshot,' jumping out of planes to put out forest fires. But it's also steady work, and you help people."

"[Firefighting is] America's sexiest job. I want to be a 'hotshot,' jumping out of planes to put out forest fires."

Wow! Jumping out of planes, I thought to myself. I'm glad my two sons (both in their early twenties) only want to be rock and jazz musicians. Later, I shared Cameron's highest ambition with my wife. She was tickled and said, "You know, we need people like Cameron to do that kind of work." She is absolutely right.

Cameron continued, "In the meantime, I think I might open a bakery and live on top of it. I want my own business while I wait for a call for the fireman's job. I think the food industry is a good choice because everyone eats. I'll own a lot of businesses. Some will sink or swim. But I'll make my million."

> "I'll own a lot of businesses. Some will sink or swim. But I'll make my million."

Then, out of nowhere, he remarked, "I've got lots of ideas—that's very ADD."

He still occasionally helps his father. "I'll make a 'house call' for my dad—that means picking up a body. I might do as many as twenty a month. He pays me $100 per call. I've always hated the business. It's gross—the bodies, the diseases, the blood—but the money is good."

He went on about school. "In high school, I went because I had to go. I'd cheat. In my first college class, a cute girl named Brittany was trying to cheat off me. I had to get it right for her. I learned that all I had to do was pay attention the first time and I'd get it." His parents had tried, unsuccessfully, to get him to do this throughout his school career, but it took a cute girl for him to have this breakthrough.

MEMORIES OF RITALIN PAST

As we discussed his memories of his visits to my office, he commented, "It wasn't that much fun coming. My sister really hated it, but I could do it. What I hated the most is when Mom would talk to you about me, because then you would find out all the bad stuff I had done."

Like Sam, I believe that Cameron never liked coming to see me. He felt pretty bad about causing problems for his family, but could never articulate that feeling. Actually, Cameron didn't really like talking at all. I also took to heart his remark about what he hated the most: what he perceived as being "told on" by his mother. Unfortunately, talking about problems is an inevitable part of trying to do something about them. But I've always made a point of meeting parents alone first to get a full history. Then, when the child participates, I remind the parents to talk directly to him or her about the issues that concern them, rather than talking exclusively to me. This decreases, at least a little, the tendency of parents to unwittingly treat their children like furniture. Cameron's reflections reinforced my commitment to this technique.

He continued on about his memories of treatment. "I always hated taking the medicine. Somebody would always ask me, especially if I did something wrong, 'Did you take your medicine?' I hated that, too. Everybody knew I took it, but it was better in high school when I took the long-acting [type]."

Cameron had hit upon another common complaint. Inevitably, when someone takes psychiatric medication and improves, then has a bad or off day, family and friends will ask, "Did you take your medicine?" Virtually all my patients who have taken psychiatric drugs—either as children or as adults—have been asked this question and they, like Cameron, hate it, because it implies that, without the medication, they can't control themselves. It diminishes the sense of competency and self-control of the person taking the drug. On some level, it potentially belittles or insults the user.

Cameron went on about his memories of Ritalin. "I could tell when I wasn't on it. When I was on it, I got through the day better. I think about using it now . . . but no. It would help me be more productive, but I don't want to take it. Just 'man up,' I say to myself. The parents who don't have kids with ADD look down upon the parents who do medicate their kids." (Cameron is generally correct about this tendency.) He went on to say that he hasn't taken Ritalin since the day he finished high school. "I'm better now because I took it then. It helped me use my head sometimes, which was better than never. I'd probably be in jail if I hadn't taken it when I was in high school."

> "I'd probably be in jail if I hadn't taken [Ritalin] when I was in high school."

I asked him about his sister, who also had problems and was sent to a residential school during her high school years. "My sister helps a company that has a search engine. She still dates trash. She had many more problems with drugs and stealing. My mom is a soldier—she kept us in line—while my dad would get more belligerent. I'm on good terms with both of them.

"In high school, I thought I could control my behavior. I liked being wilder and nuttier. I was smoking weed a lot. I drank and drove. I got caught once and stopped, but then I also got caught drinking while driving the boat. Really, I got caught most of the time. There weren't many worse things [that I otherwise got away with]. I was the loud asshole. I used to get into fights regularly—I could handle myself. Some kids didn't like me, but I always had friends."

In response to my request for his opinion on the pluses and minuses of having ADHD, Cameron said, "School, when I was younger, was the worst. It's still frustrating to go off on my own while people are talking. But I say what's on my mind. I'm straightforward and honest."

This was without a doubt the most Cameron had ever talked to me, possibly because he was getting more comfortable with himself as he got older. Though he was not terribly animated, his words and ideas had a refreshing bluntness and candor. He didn't put on airs or offer even a trace of sycophancy. That was not his style.

In that way, he was the same as he had been throughout his childhood, when his determination was viewed as stubbornness. Now, as a young adult, he seemed ready to become yet another of the dynamic entrepreneurs, or even heroes, whom this country values and honors. Every young adult enters a stage of life where they find their vocational role or career choice. Cameron and Evan both exemplify the added challenges that people with ADHD face. Their successful trajectories remind us that the range of opportunities broaden so greatly after high school. Not every ADHD child is as lucky as these two with regards to the supports and interventions they received as children. But their progress suggests that having survived an ADHD childhood, the importance of their ADHD as adults diminishes.

> Their progress suggests that having survived an ADHD childhood, the importance of their ADHD as adults diminishes.

6

. . .

With a Little Help from My Friends

Over the course of more than thirty years in behavioral-developmental pediatrics, I have found that some patients and their families hold special places in my memory and heart. I've mentioned the children in my "hall of infamy"—those whose personalities or situations were unforgettably extreme or painful. But when I recall shepherding Bobby Hall and his parents through Bobby's early childhood and into young adulthood, a far more positive connection and fondness come to mind. Perhaps "shepherd" is too strong a verb. I could choose "participate" or "experience" instead, because I'm still uncertain just how much difference a doctor can make in children's long-term outcomes. But let me tell his story and the reader can decide.

Bobby was twelve when I featured him in *Running on Ritalin*, but I had known him since March 1992, when he was seven. The following is an excerpt from the book that sums up our early interactions:

Only in the second grade, Bobby was having a terrible year and had already been suspended five times for using bad language, spitting, and losing his temper. The previous year the school psychologist gave him a full psychoeducational evaluation and felt Bobby had some of the hallmarks of ADHD but also had emotional problems. She recommended that Bobby be moved to a special class for children with severe emotional disturbances, but the Halls had resisted the idea of putting their child in such a restrictive environment.

Bobby was average in size for an almost-eight-year-old, with longish blond hair; nothing was very remarkable about his appearance. His level of physical activity seemed quite high; from the moment we were alone, he fidgeted, bounced, and squirmed, sometimes just barely maintaining contact with the chair. He was also pretty distractible, abruptly changing subjects as we talked. Or he'd look out the window at the traffic on the street or up at the ceiling vents when the air-conditioning came on.

Bobby was among the most hyperactive children I have met in my three decades of practice. His impulsivity wasn't limited to the physical world—he blurted out his thoughts and feelings as well. Quite forthright, he told me he didn't like his teacher, Mrs. Martin. She wasn't fair, he said; he hadn't been allowed to go on the last field trip. Then, extending his middle finger upward, he said, "I'm going to stop doing this. I get into trouble. Kids bug me and I give them the finger." Once he started on this topic, a lot of conflicting thoughts tumbled out. "I've got a lot of anger sometimes. I use swear words and now I swing at the kids. I try and tell the yard duty [supervisor] but she doesn't do anything. It's no big deal getting suspended. My parents don't like it." When his father got sharp with him, he said, his response was "Shut up, jerk, shitface!" He was getting pretty worked up, and I told him that swearing in the office was not a good idea.

Then, extending his
middle finger
upward, he said,
"I'm going to stop
doing this. I get into
trouble. Kids bug
me and I give them
the finger."

I feel the same way about swearing in my office today, but this was in 1992, before rap and hip-hop made the use of four-letter words common for middle schoolers. And Bobby was only seven! Aside from problems with discipline and behavior with authority figures, his conflicts with peers were a recurrent theme for Bobby and his family over the next eleven years. Only later, however, did I learn from Bobby that his lack of friendships was the most painful part of growing up with ADHD.

June, his mother, described Bobby's problems with other children: "He seems to have an incredibly short fuse. Kids tease him and no one at the school tries to stop them, as far as I can tell. The teachers and other folks at the school just seem real negative towards Bobby."

I went about helping Bobby in my typical fashion, working closely with his parents and school. In particular, I helped his parents get over any ambivalence they may have had about quick and immediate discipline. They were already using the counting method (as described in the popular parenting guide *1-2-3 Magic* by Thomas Phelan), but I believed they needed to incorporate limited physical interventions, such as physically holding Bobby in the time-out area, to make the punishment stick.

With my advice, they also used immediate rewards—including money and food—along with a kitchen timer to set specific temporal limits, both for onerous tasks (cleaning his room) and fun (playing on the computer). Over the years, his mother and I had several meetings with school personnel and managed to convey to teachers Bobby's need for timely discipline and rewards.

And then there was Ritalin. Through all my years of practice,

I have insisted that proven nondrug inter- **In particular, I**
ventions (behavioral modification and special **helped his parents**
education)be tried first. However, some chil- **get over any**
dren, like Bobby, are just so hyperactive and im- **ambivalence they**
pulsive that medication appears to be indicated **may have had**
right from the beginning of our relationship. **about quick and**
immediate
Initially, Bobby took the medication only in **discipline.**
the morning; within months, Bobby's parents
and I collectively made the decision that he also
take a dose during the lunch break at school. His afternoon behavior at school consistently deteriorated. Though children with severe
ADHD routinely took up to three daily doses of Ritalin (each of
which lasted only four hours), Bobby took just two. June felt she
could handle him at home, and with her perseverance, he could
even get homework done without medication. That way, Ritalin's
usual side effects of decreased appetite and (if taken too late in the
day) problems with falling asleep at night were minimized.

Believing that Bobby's anger could find release in play therapy,
I met with him alone. Today, I generally meet with both children
and their parents, and do very little ongoing play therapy. About
fifteen years ago, I came to the conclusion that—at least, in my
hands—weekly meetings of talk and play with young children did
not lead to changes outside the therapy room. Unless the parents
or school altered their approaches, my play and talk with the child
did little good. Many therapists may disagree with me, but in my
experience, play therapy is of limited benefit without broader
changes in the child's family or school environment.

Fortunately, Bobby was bright and had no learning problems,
and the interventions allowed him to continue in regular classes.
During his middle school years, he developed an interest and skill
in cartooning. Sonic the Hedgehog, a popular video game character

Though schoolmates came to respect his artistic ability, his friendships were limited all the way through high school.

of the early 1990s, was his favorite subject. Though schoolmates came to respect his artistic ability, his friendships were limited all the way through high school.

During that first year, I met with Bobby, alone or with his family, twenty-seven times; I doubt I would meet that frequently today. I believe I've become more "efficient"—especially with regards to decreasing weekly meetings with children by themselves. I've also learned that families actually need a longer interval between visits, more like two to three weeks ideally, to do their "homework." Thereafter, my meetings with Bobby and his parents tapered to twice a year—biannual mental health and medication "checkups." There was an occasional extra meeting or two for a crisis—Bobby failing a class in high school, for example. But overall, I maintained this routine until Bobby was eighteen and graduated. I didn't see him again until he was twenty-five and arrived for our interview.

FINDING THE PERSONAL NICHE

If I passed him a thousand times on the street, I would never have recognized him. I later asked him how much he weighed at eighteen while he was still taking Ritalin. He looked at his driver's license and told me 130 pounds. He was slightly embarrassed to say he now weighed 215 pounds. Of course, he had filled out in terms of muscle mass, but I remembered him as a slight youth.

We shook hands and moved into the office, which he said he recalled quite well. The large family room with the sectional couches was first. Then came the smaller room with large picture windows framing a view of Mount Diablo and shelves of miniature toys and a sandbox, relics of my play therapy days.

"Your building was nice and modern. I had fun here," he said, which was gratifying to hear. Committed to practicing family therapy since the start of my career, I've also tried to make sure that children weren't bored and had occasions for fun, usually by playing with toys and saving at least some time for a family game. "You were the first doctor who made a difference in my life. I had already been to a few that I felt weren't doing anything. Andy, my previous therapist, held me down, and I wanted to rip his head off."

> "Andy, my previous therapist, held me down, and I wanted to rip his head off."

We adjourned to Genova's, the Italian deli down the street. As we talked over lunch, I noticed that his speech had something of a staccato quality. Later, when reviewing *Running on Ritalin*, I came across this passage on Bobby at age seven: "[H]is way of speaking was oddly constricted: the phrases were rapid and clipped, almost mechanical or robotic, with little variation in tone and expression."

Traces of that style remained, but now his speech was livelier, animated—still quick but emotionally connected, and he made good eye contact. I believe that at age seven, his conversational style already reflected many years of negative reactions from others. I again asked him about his weight. "Too many years, especially when I was in art school, getting by with beer, pizza, and caffeine in two-liter Coke bottles." He assured me that his weight had stabilized and that he was now getting more exercise.

He wore a rainbow medallion around his neck and a small white ribbon pinned to his T-shirt. I wasn't familiar with the cause denoted by the ribbon and asked him about it. "It's a demonstration of my solidarity with the anti–Proposition 8 coalition," he told me. "You know, the anti-gay-marriage initiative in California." That comment, combined with the rainbow medallion, caused me to inquire about his sexual preference, and he confirmed that he was gay. "I was never really interested in girls. My friends were all guys, and we were the geeks. I do remember having pictures of men on my computer, though, in high school."

So Bobby was gay? I wondered how I had entirely missed this through his high school years.

So Bobby was gay? I wondered how I had entirely missed this through his high school years. When I checked my office notes later, I saw an occasional mention of girls, but Bobby was primarily entrenched in the virtually all-male 3-D computer animation crowd. Theirs was a special common-interest clique—not large, but large enough to provide a social arena for Bobby as a teenager.

It was after high school, when he attended the Academy of Art University in San Francisco, that Bobby realized his primary attraction to men. "I was so much happier there. Elementary school was the worst. Middle school and high school were better, but us geeks were still outcasts." The Academy of Art was the first place he felt like he truly fit in socially, he said; though just twenty-five miles east of San Francisco, Walnut Creek is another world, both in terms of culture and sexual mores. "I feel I could go out with women, too. But overall, I'd say I'm eighty-twenty attracted to men more than women."

I asked him how his parents reacted to his coming out. "Mom said, 'I want grandchildren.' It took them two years to become entirely comfortable with my sexual identity. Now I can have boyfriends over even when my parents are around." No serious relationships, though, he said. "The longest has been for about six to eight months. But I'm an old-school guy—no sex for sex's sake."

I asked what motivated him to become involved with the anti–Prop. 8 cause.

"The passage of Proposition 8 crossed my anger threshold. I

just felt I had to get up and do something rather than keep bitching at Fox News. I've started this Contra Costa County Equality Campaign—the Courage Campaign." (Walnut Creek is part of Contra Costa County and, as I mentioned before, is far more conservative than San Francisco.) He told me he had just run his first meeting attended by only eight people. But he wasn't in any way discouraged and felt it was a good start to his personal campaigning. I was impressed by his optimism and energy, some of Bobby's qualities that I recalled I noted even back in his high school days when I thought things were still difficult for him.

"I haven't officially graduated. I know it's been six years since high school, but taking five or six years to complete a degree isn't atypical. I really liked school. There were people from everywhere who really wanted to do something with their lives. I learned more art skills while I was there, but actually, I learned more from my mess-ups." Once again, I had a sense that Bobby really blossomed—both in terms of focus and socially—when he went to art school.

He went on to say that he had all the credits he needed to graduate but was in dispute with a professor over the completion of one of his classes; he felt the dispute was eminently solvable. Referring to the cutthroat environment of business and art, he said, "Whether you're an artist or entrepreneur, you have to know how to play the game—and it's an ugly world." I interpreted this comment as a realistic balance to Bobby's aforementioned optimism. He wasn't a Pollyanna.

"Whether you're an artist or entrepreneur, you have to know how to play the game— and it's an ugly world."

Bobby still lived at home with his parents. His domestic arrangements were not so unusual for mid-twenties types trying to live in the very expensive Bay Area. "My parents are away a lot," he commented. Bobby's father, Bill, is a hospital director in Southern California, and June frequently spends time during the week in

Palm Springs. "I can have a party with them around—granted, for me, a party is pretty low-key: four or five people coming over. I still clash some with them [his parents] over small things. However, if

"There's too much going on in the real world to spend much time in front of a screen."

I were to be in a serious relationship, I'd want my own place. At my parents' home, I do have a great studio for painting. I still do some gaming with my friends, but there's too much going on in the real world to spend much time in front of a screen."

We had talked about many subjects but hadn't yet spoken about Ritalin, so I asked him if he was currently taking any medication. He said that he wasn't, that he'd stopped after graduating from high school. I remembered that much of Bobby's hyperactivity had disappeared during the middle school years, but he'd continued on the medication throughout high school to help keep him on track academically. Once he entered art school, where the classes themselves interested him, he no longer needed the medication.

RECALLING RITALIN

Going on about his memories of taking Ritalin, he noted, "We tried the medication and I could see it made a difference, and everyone told me so. At the time [age seven] I didn't give it too much thought. I remember getting the pills [the second dose of the day] in the back room of the school. It was only a mild hassle. In my younger years, I knew I had a huge problem focusing. Now kids are just getting Ritalin for nothing. 'Ritalin—here, take it'—without the deliberation and thought that went into the decision for me.

"I did have some rebellious feelings about the medication in middle and high school but I never felt coerced. We lowered the dose in high school. But after high school I said no. I occasionally wondered about its effect on my brain and development. I once had a friend who took 'meth' [an illegal amphetamine very similar to legal stimulants] and I learned a lot from watching him. I saw a lot of the same patterns I once had.

"The only side effect I experienced was appetite suppression, and it didn't bother me. I really started gaining weight about three years after I stopped the medication. But my experience [the medication] took place within a controlled environment. I think it was appropriate in my case. These days, it's 'I'm stressed,' and they take a Zoloft. No, if you're working too hard, you should regulate your environment and what drugs you put into your system. I felt a trained professional did a good evaluation and treatment. There is no magic pill. My experience was positive."

> "These days, it's 'I'm stressed,' and they take a Zoloft."

I was struck by the contrast between his feelings about his experience taking medication and how he views current practices. His views strikingly matched mine, even though he had been the patient and I the doctor.

As we wrapped up the interview, he asked if I'd like to see his sketchbook, and of course I said I would. He showed me detailed pencil and charcoal drawings of scenes from Italy and France. "Companies like Pixar are much more interested in people who have original art ideas and skills rather than computer savvy," he said. "The computer stuff can be taught more easily than the other."

By the end of our conversation, I recognized the old Bobby. He was lively, animated, and spirited—all the good qualities of personality that the "disorder" of ADHD confers. Throughout his trials and struggles, Bobby maintained an ineffable but enthusiastic intensity. Now in his mid-twenties, he was able to target his energetic intensity to the areas he wanted.

CHECKING IN WITH JUNE

Russell Barkley's research indicated that parents generally confirmed their grown children's observations, and talking to the parents of my interviewees wasn't on my agenda. But puzzled about missing early signs of Bobby's homosexuality, and curious about how it might have related to his overall social struggles, especially in high school, I decided to check in with his mother, June.

She wanted to talk about other things first. "Art school was great for him, and me. It was the first time I didn't have to check or coordinate his activities and responsibilities. *Hey, I'm done,* I said to myself. The main thing was that he was passionate about it. Now, it's the anti-Prop. 8 campaign. He's getting these groups together. He's been to meetings in LA. When he talks about it, he shines. He's acting responsibly!

> "Art school was great for him, and me. It was the first time I didn't have to check or coordinate his activities and responsibilities."

"He has kept his close friends from elementary and high school. He struggled more in high school when he didn't have as much to relate to as the other kids, but in art school, they shared many more common interests." I thought of *The Ugly Duckling*—the classic story of a swan who, as a youngster, is rejected by farmyard ducks and geese but then, as an adult, meets other swans and lives happily ever after.

"Now he's about to graduate from school. He'll do the ceremony. He really doesn't want to go to graduation but he's said, 'I'll do it for you, Ma.' I'd like him to lose some weight before the graduation." When I commented on how much weight he's gained, she said, "Oh, he's just like his father. They're both overweight. The medication definitely kept his weight down."

I had to ask her. "June, about Bobby's gayness. I seemed to miss it entirely. What did you know, or see?"

She wasn't at all fazed by my question. "In high school, he did go to the prom but it was more with friends. Near the end of high school and beginning of college, he seemed shy. He was scared of girls. He was confused. I thought, 'He'll find someone to relate to.' It's been only in the last eighteen months that his sexual identity has become clear to us. I didn't see anything in his growing up—I found *Playboy* magazines in his room."

June continued, "We're supportive of whatever Bobby wants. I mean, it couldn't be any other way. He's our child. I wouldn't have chosen this path—there are some crazy people out there. But we love him unconditionally."

While I had her on the telephone, I asked about her memories of Ritalin. "In the beginning, the idea of giving him the medicine was a problem for us. Even just thinking about it. You allayed our fears. I was willing to try it. It changed his life. He could function normally. I remember he said 'I'm not the same bad boy anymore.'

"But we also got a lot of information and insights from you about dealing with him and the teachers. Before that, we were flying blind. This was the way he was and is, and we were just so glad we found a doctor who could help us make good decisions about him. We've come so far. Bobby is a character. So many neighbors have told me he is a wonderful guy."

ADDRESSING THE ADHD SOCIAL PARIAH

I shouldn't have been surprised (but yet I was) to learn from Bobby himself—not from his parents, teachers, or doctors—that social connections or problems with his peers were both the most important and the most painful memories of growing up with ADHD. When I talk to children in my office and ask them what they would identify as their biggest problem (I often substitute the words "most annoying" for "biggest problem"), trouble with friends—either making them or keeping them—is generally number one. Parents and teachers are also concerned about children's social life, but generally rate school performance, compliance, and arguments at home as the number one problems.

I have come to appreciate the critical importance of social connections and intimate peer relationships to the happiness of these children, now grown.

In the course of these interviews, I have come to appreciate the critical importance of social connections and intimate peer relationships to the happiness of these children, now grown. School performance and arguing with his mother and father were predominant problems for Bobby through the years I knew him as a patient. Yet in our contemporary conversation, he barely mentioned either to me.

In Bobby's case, it's hard to separate the social challenges he faced as a result of his extreme hyperactivity and impulsivity compared to his later homosexual interests. I believe the former actually had a more profound impact, especially during his early school years and especially before he had the benefits of the medication and a concerted, coordinated behavioral plan.

Researchers William Pelham (SUNY Buffalo) and Steve Hinshaw (UC Berkeley) have conducted extensive research into the peer relationship problems of school-age children with ADHD. Both men run special full-day summer camp programs that incorporate "normal" children as well as those with ADHD. Several of their studies have included camper ratings of themselves and of the other children of their group—essentially, popularity polls.

Tellingly, children with more severe ADHD are consistently rated the lowest in popularity, primarily for "breaking the rules" and for being "bad sports." Even the ADHD children rate their ADHD peers the lowest, a sign that it's easier to recognize problems in others than

Children with more severe ADHD are consistently rated the lowest in popularity.

to do something about them in yourself. The speed with which these opinions form—within the first three days of an eight-week program—is also intriguing. Despite minute-by-minute monitoring and immediate reinforcement from trained college-age counselors, campers with ADHD are still at the bottom of the popularity poll at the end of the camp program.

As we've seen, children (and adults) are complex, rarely reducible to a single diagnostic label like ADHD. In fact, most of the campers with ADHD had also been diagnosed with other conditions, most commonly oppositional defiant disorder. Additionally, many displayed signs of a lowered self-image, which is like adding fuel to the fire of ADHD.

When you feel bad about yourself, you often try too hard with your peers, want to be in charge, and need events to go your way (for example, losing is more difficult to handle gracefully). This often results in a cascade of emotions and reactions: negative feelings lead to negative actions lead to negative reactions from others lead to more negative feelings. Stubbornness or anxiety only makes the peer problems worse.

June's comments about Bobby's long-ago high and instant reactivity to being teased are a reflection of this cycle. It can be very difficult to interrupt this pattern of negativity. For one, parents and teachers miss many important peer interactions. Reviewing proper behavior ("Ignore the teasing," for example) is of little benefit; the impulsive child already knows the consequences but struggles in the present to utilize that information.

Role playing may sometimes help a bit. My advice to parents is that they practice, practice, practice with children in situations in which adults are ready to intervene and reinforce both appropriate and inappropriate behavior with immediate rewards and consequences (if necessary). I'm not certain what helped Bobby break the negative peer relationship cycle. June and Bill would probably attribute it to their own firming up and becoming more effective with their discipline. Learning to accept parents' limits helps children learn to accept limits (such as taking turns) with their peers.

Currently, I often recommend that parents play board games with their children.

Currently, I often recommend that parents play board games with their children, building in specific rewards and consequences for good or bad sportsmanship. For example, after one warning for whining when losing, the second time, the child (or adult, for that matter) loses his or her turn. Alternatively, gracefully handling going down the longest slide in Chutes and Ladders might garner an extra turn.

Closely supervising playdates and being prepared to intervene, first with a reminder and then with action (such as a temporary time-out, in which the parent of the ADHD child replaces him in play with the friend) is another suggestion I often offer parents. Then, there are supervised group activities—from team sports and scouting groups to more therapeutic pursuits. Any group therapy for children includes group playtime during which behavior is monitored and reinforced, much like the summer camp programs mentioned earlier.

Finally, there's medication. Besides its concentrating effects, perhaps more importantly, Ritalin makes people more methodical, more deliberate, and less impulsive. I tell children, "Ritalin gives you a fraction of a second longer to consider taking the wiser choice or action." Bobby didn't participate in groups, but I think, for him,

Ritalin was extremely helpful in decreasing— though not eliminating—his impulsive reactions to other children.

When it comes to one's sense of self-worth and, for that matter, of one's worth to others, it also helps to have a passion or skill. When Bobby was seven, no one could have predicted his growing interest and skill in the graphic arts. But by the time he was eleven, Bobby was drawing elaborate cartoons of his favorite video characters that charmed me, his parents, and other children. These skills morphed to a focus on computer graphics and animation by age thirteen. Yes, he was one of the geeks, but he had interests and passions that were shared by other kids.

"Ritalin gives you a fraction of a second longer to consider taking the wiser choice or action."

I'm not sure how much of a role Bobby's same-sex proclivities played in his pre–high school social problems. I believe much of Bobby's hyperactivity and impulsivity had disappeared by the time conflicted or confused feelings about same-sex attraction appeared in his life. Certainly, Bobby could have struggled peer-wise and socially in high school because of his growing awareness of his sexual preferences. June notes that he seemed shyer late in high school, but I don't think his ADHD was playing much of a role then, compared to, say, his difficulty with completing assignments, which remained a problem until art school.

However, without a doubt, the San Francisco art scene experience allowed Bobby's personality to fully flower. The Bobby I met at twenty-five was the happiest Bobby I had known, and perhaps the most overtly happy adult I met during my interviews for this book. Once again, this might have been simply because Bobby was always pretty intense and, by middle school, fairly impervious— he let his troubles roll off his back (to the enduring consternation of his parents).

Bobby still is not on his own financially. He has yet to show that he can earn a living that will allow him to live independently, either by himself or with a partner of his choice. However, I am confident that Bobby will be happy, far happier than I would have predicted when I knew him as a child and adolescent. He has found his niches, both personal and professional. He has grown into a beautiful swan.

7

. . .

Bad Outcomes

Considering the Limits of Treatment

Professionally, I feel I've been very lucky over the course of my career. As far as I know, only a handful of the children I've treated have experienced an outright disaster in their lives. Though defining a "bad" outcome is as tricky as defining mental "health," most would agree that felony convictions, jail, alcohol and drug abuse, and suicide would qualify as bad outcomes.

I, like most doctors in private practice, have no formal or consistent follow-up contact with patients once they leave my practice. However, on two occasions, mothers of my former patients have contacted me.

The first was Cathy, grieving over the suicide of her son, John, who hung himself at age twenty-two after his girlfriend left him and took their child with her. I had been involved with John and his parents six years earlier, when he was sixteen, for about a year. To this day, I remember an episode that took place in my office; it was the only time in three decades I've ever had to call the police during a session. John's parents announced that they intended to hospital-ize him. When he heard the news, he bolted from the meeting, and then returned with a tire iron in his hand, threatening to break down my office door to get at his father. When the police arrived, he meekly surrendered. Five years later, I learned from Cathy that John had barely finished high school, was dealing drugs, and con-tinued to have violent episodes with his girlfriend.

The second mother, Joan, returned ten years after I had worked with her daughter, Carla, who was sixteen at the time, and her fam-ily. By the time she was twenty-six, Carla was a habitual drug abuser, and Joan was raising her two boys, ages four and two. Joan had concerns about the boys' long-term future—primarily, Carla's ge-netic legacy. Both mothers, Joan and Cathy, were struggling with a sense of guilt, wondering what more they—or anyone else—could have done for their children.

A PRISONER RETURNS

Other updates are more roundabout. Roughly seven years after I had last seen Kevin O'Rourke professionally, I received a telephone call out of the blue from a woman who identified herself only by her first name. She asked me if I knew Kevin and had written about him in *Running on Ritalin*. Though I didn't acknowledge knowing Kevin, I asked why she wanted to know. "Kevin stabbed me in the back with a screwdriver and he's in jail," she said. "He wants me to believe that he has these prob-lems and was in your book."

"Kevin stabbed me in the back with a screwdriver and he's in jail."

I told her that, for reasons of confidentiality, I couldn't answer her question one way or the other. Clearly annoyed and frustrated by my response, she hung up. The call disturbed me enough to get in touch with Kevin's mother, Janice. She briefly confirmed the story, but her short, tight answers made me feel she really didn't want to talk about her son's current troubles.

Months later, I received a release that gave me permission to speak about Kevin to a forensic psychiatrist hired by the state. When we talked, I learned that Kevin had been convicted of a crime and that issues of pharmaceutical treatment and the length of his sentence were still unresolved. This was as much as I knew about Kevin's adult life until I spoke to him for this book.

Here's some of what I wrote about Kevin in *Running on Ritalin*:

I followed . . . Kevin O'Rourke for nine years, beginning in 1989, when he was seven. He was one of those kids for whom Ritalin made a huge difference; I don't know if it saved his life, but when I first saw him, he was about to get expelled from school for the second time. His single mother, Janice, had been reported to the local child-abuse agency for allegedly hitting him. She also had a younger son and daughter and little control over any of the three; their family life was chaotic. But Kevin was her major headache.

Kevin was exquisitely sensitive to Ritalin. He was very bright, but without the medication, he was one of the most hyperactive and impulsive children I'd ever met. His thought patterns and conversation were extremely tangential, jumping from one subject to the next with the barest of connections.

Kevin's was not a simple case of ADHD. An anxious child, he worried that his performance was inadequate, yet he rarely admitted this openly. In fact, he almost always denied having any problems—a clear sign that he was too scared to acknowledge them. It's not unusual for children to engage in denial as a form of coping . . . Kevin "forgot" to take his pill [regularly] . . . inevitably prompting a call from the school.

Unlike many children who grow out of their hyperactivity en-

tirely [during adolescence], he remained somewhat fidgety and impulsive. Meanwhile, though, he matured into a tall, strong young man who performed very well in school. He could read twelfth-grade-level material on entering high school and was a whiz in science. He still attended special-ed classes, and once admitted to me that he was frightened of giving up that support. While Kevin continued to reiterate that he didn't want to take Ritalin, the prescriptions would invariably be filled.

I haven't heard from him recently, but I suspect that he did eventually stop taking medication. Perhaps he'll get back in touch when he's in his twenties and reconsidering its benefits. Or he may have found a calling in which he can perform without its assistance. I'd like to know in either case.

I included Kevin in *Running on Ritalin* to highlight the drug's dramatic effect. Though I wrote that Janice was single, she was, in fact, married to Jeff, who was away on a long-term assignment for the military and returned home only twice a year for a two-week interval. This effectively made Janice a single mother during the first three years we were in contact. Once Jeff was back in the home full-time, the level of conflict between Kevin and his parents increased.

This is a complicated story. Janice was often depressed to the point that the requirements of daily life (work and parenting) were a huge burden for her. Jeff, like his son, was highly intelligent, and had been engaged in military intelligence. Diagnosed with ADD himself, Jeff also took Ritalin at one point in my treatment of the family.

But mostly, it was the level of conflict in the house that made an enduring impression on me. I vividly recall a meeting during which I had to break up a physical fight between Kevin and Jeff. Kevin had been sassing both parents, and Jeff ordered him into the corner. Given that Kevin was fifteen at the time, a time-out of that nature seemed inappropriate. When Kevin refused, Jeff grabbed him and shoved him up against the wall. When I yelled "Stop!" Jeff backed off. This ugly encounter highlighted the family's ongoing intensity.

I vividly recall a meeting during which I had to break up a physical fight between Kevin and his father.

In 2000, I also saw Kevin's younger brother, Joe, who at twelve was also challenging his mother and teachers. I learned from Janice that she and Jeff were considering separating; then she became pregnant and had a fourth child. The arguing between the couple continued, and finally, Jeff left and moved to eastern Washington State.

That's all the information I had when I tried to locate Kevin to talk to him for this book. The phone numbers I had for Janice had been disconnected; then on a lark, I tried Information in the area Janice had lived the last time. When I called, a male voice answered the phone. It turned out to be her ex-husband, Jeff, who told me that he and Janice were living together once again, at least temporarily. When I said I was trying to reach Kevin, he replied, "He's right here. Let me give him the phone." And it was that easy.

I explained the project to Kevin, and he agreed to meet with me without any conditions. Though I was pleased, I was also nervous. I really wanted to have Kevin's memories in the book. His experience, I thought, would highlight a less-than-good outcome, which I thought was important for balance. But I had never had an in-depth conversation with someone who had spent time in prison. I was sensitive about both his feelings and the perception of exploitation.

Therefore, I anticipated our meeting with more apprehension than I'd felt about any of the other interviews. As I climbed the stairs to my office, I thought I had about a quarter of an hour until my appointment with Kevin, but when I got to the top of the stairs,

I saw a large man who appeared to be in his late twenties sitting on the window ledge. He had a manicured mustache and goatee, and wore dark sunglasses, a baseball cap, and a sweatshirt with the hood down. When he said, "Hello, Dr. Diller," and gave me a wry smile, I realized that it was Kevin.

Once again, I kept my shock at a former patient's size—both height and weight—to myself. In their late teens, all of the guys had weighed about 135 pounds and were as thin as rails. Now, as young adults, they were pushing 180 pounds or more, some of which could be explained by a normal filling-out during the maturation process. Still, I was coming to the conclusion that when they were younger, their meds had kept their eating in check and their weight low.

Because I had forgotten the keys to my office (was I that nervous?), we weren't able to go in. I mentioned that I was disappointed, but he didn't seem to care. When I said something about the sandbox toys, he spoke up. "I remember Jeff O'Rourke." He had given one of the figures, a state police officer, his father's name. At that point, he had seen very little of his father for nearly three years. Kevin used this figure in his surprisingly violent play therapy stories, which he enacted over and over again when we met during those early years.

TOYS AND PILLS

He went on to say that he also recalled the Etch A Sketch and stacking rings, waiting room toys I've kept (and repeatedly replaced) over the years, as well as a soldier with a rocket launcher, a World War II toy figure that he regularly employed in his wars in the sand, "and that game, Truth or Consequences." I told him he was likely referring to the Talking, Feeling, Doing Game, a classic psychotherapy tool I've used with kids and families almost as long as I've been in practice.

On the way to lunch, we began to reminisce. Kevin commented that he remembered Dan McCarthy, the social worker who had worked with Kevin, his family, and me for a decade when Kevin was enrolled in a special program for disturbed children at the Marchus School. "Dan was a real good guy," I said, and Kevin agreed, then noted that he had started at Marchus when he was in the second grade. I had forgotten that he had been placed in a special education setting so early in his life.

> "I never noticed that they were working, except that I didn't eat."

When we sat down, I began the interview with his memories of the medications he took. "I know I started with the yellow ones," he said, and I told him they were 5-milligram Ritalin tablets. "Then I went to the green [10 milligrams] and then the blue ones [20 milligrams]. I never really understood what it was until much later. I knew it was behavior-related. I never noticed that they were working, except that I didn't eat. I would run for the pantry at the end of the day when they wore off. I wished that they made a coating on the pill that would have made them easier to swallow. They *are* basically methamphetamine."

"What about taking the pills at school?" I asked.

"The other kids would say, 'Who *are* these kids [who are different]?' I was teased sometimes, but about the same compared to normal kids. But others [parents, teachers] told me it was doing good. You know, the last time I was tested, my IQ was 111. By high school, I had figured out what the medicine was supposed to do, but I didn't like being chained to a bottle. At that point, I didn't want to take it anymore, but I had to because of my parents. I stopped at eighteen. I said, 'I'm not

> "By high school, I had figured out what the medicine was supposed to do, but I didn't like being chained to a bottle."

taking it anymore.' I wanted to join the military and I was sick of taking it. My dad was in the Navy for twenty years, an ocean systems analyst in antisubmarine warfare."

"They'd push me too far and it was 'Screw you! I'm not doing anything!'"

He reflected about high school. "They always seemed to make the same mistake with me, believing that I would do [what I was forced to do]. It happened three times. They'd push me too far and it was 'Screw you! I'm *not doing anything*!' I remember I was in metal shop when the teacher pushed me too far the first time.

"I graduated from high school with a regular diploma, then worked for a fast-food place for six months. It was boring as hell. I'm generally intolerant of stupid people. I knew my job, so when a guest manager bugged me, I told her to shut up. This was a little upsetting . . . I was fired." He recounted this with a straight face, and I remembered that this was typical of Kevin's understated humor.

"I enlisted in the Army—they took me despite my ADHD and Ritalin because they said I was okay as long as I was off it for a period of time. We [my parents and I] fudged some of that time. That turned out not to help my cause." When I asked what he meant, he explained.

"We had a food problem that was causing an ant infestation in the barracks. I didn't respond fast enough to the drill sergeant and was told I had an 'attitude problem.' When he gave me remedial PT [extra exercises], I called him an SOB. They started looking at my records and then sent me to a military psychologist. 'We're going to send you home for two years and you can reapply.' They discharged me under 'false enlistment.' I was in the Army for about five months."

When I asked him how he felt about the military overall, he observed, "Military bureaucrats are pencil pushers. God forbid you have

someone who could kill someone," then continued, "Getting kicked out of the military, I
experienced as my first major failure—it
sucked. I was home for a month or two when
Mom and Dad's marriage finally disinte-
grated. I said, 'What's going on is not all Dad's
fault.' That's when she said, 'You're out, too.' I wound up going with
Dad to Spokane.

"Getting kicked out of the military, I experienced as my first major failure—it sucked."

"I got a job a Kmart and didn't like that either. But that's where
I met Jeannie [who was about forty]; I began working for her, washing dogs. We had a sort of relationship—we were drinking partners
for about six months. Then I got a job with Hart Seed Company,
which I liked, but the job ended when the harvest was over. I then
did Marie Callender's, washing dishes, and graduated to prep cook
for eleven months. I got fed up with the bosses, who blamed us [for
everything] . . . I stuck the knife in them." He didn't realize he was
using a metaphor for his later crime. "I was in charge of the brunch
tables and corporate was coming. I told them I'd [set up the tables]
in the morning, and then left things unprepared intentionally. They
were screwed and I was fired again."

This pattern of multiple jobs and short-term employment was the
same as that demonstrated by those in Barkley's H+ group who were
in their twenties and thirties—this was the group Barkley felt still
met the full criteria for active and impairing ADHD as adults. In my
opinion, Kevin, too, was clearly still functioning with a significant
ADHD problem.

He continued with his employment saga, which included another
stint at Hart Seed, then a construction company, where he dug out
basements—hard physical labor—until the company closed down.
At that point, he moved back in with his mother and helped out with
his younger sister. When I asked how he earned a living at that point,
he didn't want to talk about it; I suspected he'd been dealing drugs.

"Like when I was in jail, we got hold of some meth. Everyone was running around with their eyes bugging out and jabbering. I did two lines and went to sleep."

I asked him about methamphetamine, because it's a commonly abused drug in rural areas and he had a long history of using Ritalin, an amphetamine variant. "Meth doesn't do anything for me. Like when I was in jail, we got hold of some meth. Everyone was running around with their eyes bugging out and jabbering. I did two lines and went to sleep."

A VIOLENT ACT AND ITS CONSEQUENCES

I was a little apprehensive as we approached his crime and subsequent incarceration, and suspected that he was building a story to explain how he had come to stab Jeannie.

"I'd been living with Jeannie again for a couple of months. I was doin' weed and drinking like a fish. I had been functioning like a big capacitor—I loaded up on everything. Now, suddenly, everything was going out the other way. I was drunk and we had an argument about something. She kicked me out of the house. She was trying to rationalize—'We're saving our relationship'—but it drove me crazy. I had the screwdriver in my hand as I was gathering my tools. I left a gash in her shoulder. She called the cops. I left. They caught me. I went to jail. I didn't call anyone, but Dad showed up."

I asked him how he felt after he stabbed Jeannie and found himself in jail. Not surprisingly, he said he had been frightened. "What the hell just happened? I was disoriented—I'm trying to figure it out . . . okay, this is how it works, then—getting angry as the legal system plods along. Jeannie knew several judges and my first attorney. 'You're screwed,' I thought. I backed out of my first plea deal. After that, my attorney withdrew. I eventually pled guilty to robbery, kidnapping, and assault. I was given sixty-eight months and served forty-two."

As he told me of his time in prison from age twenty-three to twenty-seven, he mostly talked about where and when he was incarcerated rather than about his feelings. I asked him what he'd learned from his prison experience.

"Everyone has a point of view. You stay in your groups. Black with black, Hispanic with Hispanic. Your business is your business. Stay out of their business. Mostly it's people trying to do their time. I went along with it and minded my own business. In the process, I got points with the inmates and points with the guards. I saw it as a game and I wasn't going to take the bait."

> "I went along with it and minded my own business. In the process, I got points with the inmates and points with the guards."

He continued: "I'm a little more patient. I now take the sniper's view. I can wait until I can do maximum damage. I choose my time." I was distressed— this is what he learned from almost four years in prison? To wait in ambush so the attack is more effective? I felt sad but tried not to reveal that to him.

Kevin went on to say that he didn't feel that the Bay Area was his home anymore. His family had moved on with their lives, and all his friends were in Spokane. Most of his time was spent playing video games.

"My ADHD, it's still there. When I'm tired, I can't pay attention to anything. It is what it is. . . . Sometimes, being me sucks, other times it's a load of fun. The medication served its purpose for the time it was there. I don't have that service anymore. I don't need that service anymore."

When I asked him if he felt his time with me had been helpful,

"I'm a little more patient. I now take the sniper's view. I can wait until I can do maximum damage. I choose my time."

he said, "You pointed us in a direction. We did a lot of work with the anger issues, which mitigated situations which could have been worse." I thought to myself, *He used the word "mitigate," which is probably not heard that often in a prison environment.* Kevin was smart, but what had come of it?

Driving him back to the train station, I asked him what he would ideally like to do in the future. "I want to be a handyman. No, more than that—a general contractor. I have a record so I'm hard to hire. But if I'm a contractor and do the work, no one asks questions." At the station, I wished him well and thanked him, and we said good-bye.

ADHD + ODD = BIPOLAR?

Like the mothers of my three "bad outcome" patients, I wonder if I could have done more for Kevin and his family. I worked with them—at times, intensely—for nine years. He took Ritalin, up to three times a day, from age seven to seventeen. And yet, his anger and impulsivity, combined with substance use, led to the attack on his girlfriend and, ultimately, jail time. In some ways, he came through prison relatively unscarred; it doesn't appear, for example, that he was sexually abused. Still, his insights about the time he spent inside and his future goals were disturbing and limited, given his high intelligence. I am less surprised than sad and disappointed.

The long-term data on children with ADHD and anger issues is very discouraging. Those who are oppositional, challenge authority regularly, and act angry are often categorized with oppositional defiant disorder, or ODD. Adolescents who frequently break the law are often diagnosed with conduct disorder (CD), which also includes behavior criteria such as "cruel to animals." While not all kids with ODD go on to meet criteria for CD as adolescents, the large majority of kids with CD display signs of ODD as younger children. Finally, antisocial personality disorder (ASPD) is the label assigned to career criminals, who also often begin with ODD.

I'm not sure how helpful these categories are, apart from labeling and categorizing certain kinds of kids. These diagnoses are assigned to individual children, but their caregivers, schools, and neighborhoods also play a role. My experience is that these children challenge their parents and schools over limits that are inconsistently or ineffectively monitored and enforced. Eventually, parents get very angry, and emotional, verbal, and physical abuse are often routine parts of family life.

In all fairness, these kids are not easy. As I've said, persistence— which I've also called "determination" or "stubbornness"—and intensity of expression of feeling (especially anger) are temperament qualities that call for a higher degree of parental competency and confidence in setting and enforcing the family's rules of compliance. Add an impulsivity component to the personality of either the child or the parents and you have a recipe for big trouble. Some researchers feel there should actually be a separate diagnostic category for children meeting both ADHD and ODD criteria. Their lifetime trajectory is so much more negative than pure ADHD, or ADD with learning problems, that early intensive intervention, drug and nondrug, seems imperative.

I'm certain that in today's diagnostic jungle, Kevin would have been characterized early on as having pediatric bipolar disorder (PBD). This diagnosis was unheard of in chil-

> Some researchers feel there should actually be a separate diagnostic category for children meeting both ADHD and ODD criteria.

dren in 1989 when I first met Kevin. But beginning in the mid-1990s, many top child psychiatric researchers began to vigorously promote this diagnosis for teens and elementary-school-age children.

Some doctors claim that they can determine this diagnosis in children as young as two, but I have never felt comfortable assigning it even to teens, not to mention elementary- or middle-school-age children. There are just too many uncertainties about a child's future to saddle him or her with that burden.

Such pronouncements—along with coincident (and significant) conflict-of-interest scandals—have led to a major push-back from child psychiatry's officialdom. The American Academy of Child and Adolescent Psychiatry has made it clear that this diagnosis should be bestowed only rarely on children under thirteen and may not be given to children under six. The next version of the *DSM* is unlikely to support the legitimacy of the PBD diagnosis for preteens. Instead, a new category, temper dysregulation disorder (TDD), is being proposed.

While only the outlines of this category are available for evaluation at this time, my first reactions are positive, because at least a child isn't labeled with a lifelong disorder. On the other hand, I'm concerned that kids who are just intense will still be weighed down with a psychiatric diagnosis. I remain deeply skeptical that this category will lead to any substantive changes in the way frontline child psychiatrists treat these problems, which tends to be with antipsychotic, heavily sedating medications that come with serious side effects.

PERSONALITY AND THE LIMITS OF INTERVENTION

But I can understand why, at university-based clinics, doctors would be searching for and using any intervention, drug or otherwise, to make a difference in children with combined ADHD-ODD problems. Their prognosis is so discouraging. James H. Satterfield is a child psychiatrist associated with the University of California, Irvine. He and his colleagues conducted a study of children diagnosed with both ADHD and ODD that started in the 1970s and followed them for thirty years. The results were published in 2007.

His clinic was strongly committed to employing psychosocial interventions (child and family therapy, special education where necessary). Some of these children received three years of only counseling and special ed, some received just Ritalin, and one group received both treatments. Then, over the years, Satterfield checked in on his subjects to see how they were faring.

At the fifteen-year follow-up, when the study participants were in their early twenties, there seemed to be cause for hope. It appeared that the groups that had received the intensive psychosocial interventions (with or without Ritalin) did somewhat better than the Ritalin-alone group in terms of finishing high school and avoiding juvenile delinquency and substance abuse.

However, in checking the records of these individuals thirty years later, the researchers found significantly higher rates of arrest, conviction, and incarceration among all the study subjects as compared to community controls. It didn't matter whether these adults had been given the Cadillac treatment of Ritalin and psychosocial interventions or just the medication alone. Satterfield conceded that the extra treatments hadn't made a difference, and mused whether starting family therapy earlier (for the study, children had been enrolled between the ages of six and twelve) would have made any difference.

Could early and intense nondrug and drug interventions make a difference in these

> The researchers found significantly higher rates of arrest, conviction, and incarceration among all the study subjects as compared to community controls.

children's lives? This is the case made by those advocating early aggressive drug interventions in children as young as toddlers, whether one calls their problems bipolar disorder or not. However, our dysfunctional medical delivery system, especially for the poor, results in children without the benefit of family or school interventions being prescribed not just Ritalin-type drugs, but medications such as Risperdal and Zyprexa—both of which are heavily sedating and can cause massive amounts of weight gain and even diabetes.

PBD wasn't a consideration for Kevin when I first met him. Given his high degree of hyperactivity and impulsivity, early and continuous Ritalin use made sense. Weekly individual and family therapy went on for nearly three years, and then periodically when a crisis arose. Kevin was in an excellent special ed program from second grade all the way through high school. Perhaps things might have turned out worse for him without these supports and interventions. Nevertheless, considering his mistakes and likely future left me feeling sad and impotent.

CHOOSING ANOTHER PATH

When I was going through my records of the mid-1990s searching for the children who were in *Running on Ritalin*, I came across Daniel's chart. His name and the details of his problems brought up memories of a child who, even in the early 1990s, had been given a multiplicity of medications to address what I would call an ADHD-ODD situation, but whom many doctors today would diagnose as PBD or TDD. I checked out the details. Here are some of my chart notes from the first visit in 1994, when Daniel was nine and in the third grade:

Things are better than three months ago. Still with anger outbursts but more easy-going, more self-control currently. Does okay at

school but a big problem at home. Adopted age 3 months. Dx'ed
[diagnosed] with ADHD in 1991. Began Ritalin at age six. Lithium
3/93, clonidine 7/93, Prozac 12/93. Also Choline Cl for bedtime
wetting, L-tyrosine for depression. Ca/Mg/Zinc tablets. Not taking
Ritalin at this time.

While "things were better," Daniel's parents had come in because
of his regular and colossal tantrums at home over minor limit-setting
issues such as turning off the television or putting toys away. The
panoply of psychiatric drugs used with this boy strongly suggested
the parents' sense of powerlessness—their sense that Daniel's problems were not within their, or even his, control. "It must be biological," his history, in essence, said, which made their search for doctors
and a drug answer understandable, and mind
you, this was the early 1990s, when this kind
of drug history was extremely unusual, which
is probably why I so vividly remembered
Daniel twenty years later.

> The panoply of
> psychiatric drugs
> used with this boy
> strongly suggested
> the parents' sense
> of powerlessness.

At the very first family visit, which included his parents, Heidi and Frank, along
with his older (also adopted) brother, Francis, I could see an intense connection and overidentification between Heidi and Daniel.
Heidi, who had strong sympathy for her son's problems at school
and at home, simultaneously felt frustrated and angry about his
limit testing and tantrums. Frank was more distant (literally—he
traveled a great deal for work), holding Daniel to a higher standard than did Heidi; he was frustrated with both of them for the
way they "carried on."

Initially, I worked primarily with the parents (which no one had
done prior to me) to get them on the same page in terms of discipline. I especially supported Heidi as she sorted through her mixed
feelings, which she needed to do in order to effectively discipline

Daniel in an emotionally calm and even fashion. I also stopped most of Daniel's medications, but reinstituted Ritalin because he was impulsive and inattentive in my office and at school. His school performance improved, as did the family atmosphere.

As things got better, Daniel wanted to stop the Ritalin. However, when he would try to go without it, academic and behavior problems would crop up again, leading to his reconnection with the drug. Here are some notes from my last entry on Daniel, from May 1998:

> *Started rocky in new school but with the aid of a daily college student tutor, managed decent parent-satisfying grades. Has friends and is playing on the select soccer team. He is clear the medication allows him to concentrate and get his work done better at school and at home. He looks a bit thinner and weight gain has been an issue. Transfer care to general pediatrician.*

I choose to include Daniel in this book because I wanted to talk to another boy who today would have been categorized ADHD-ODD or PBD-TDD. Daniel met me at my office during a lunch break. He told me that, in general, he didn't like going to the doctor (me included). He did remember the sandbox and the toys, but otherwise didn't initially comment to any degree on the things we did together.

I was planning to take him to a better-than-average hamburger joint, but he demurred, saying it would be noisy. When he suggested the most expensive Italian restaurant in town, I was surprised and said I thought it would be too slow and stuffy. Then he suggested a newer restaurant that I had never been to, so I said okay. I thought it was interesting that Daniel could be so forward in his requests.

The place *was* more upscale and stuffy than I would have

thought he liked, but otherwise, it was fine—and indeed quieter than the hamburger joint. We sat down and I started asking him questions, beginning with what he was currently doing.

"I've just finished six months of the Sheriff's Academy. It puts me in an excellent place to now apply for law enforcement positions. I'm stoked. I liked everything I learned. There were some officers directly above me who weren't very good teachers. They just broke us down but never built us up."

He looked directly at me as we spoke, but what struck me was his relatively flat tone, even when talking about things that seemed important to him. I tried to connect this twenty-four-year-old man to the child I had known twelve years earlier. Compared to the three other young men I'd already interviewed, I felt only a minimum degree of familiarity with Daniel. Somehow, this made the experience different and slightly more difficult. I felt I still somehow "knew" the others, but my memories of Daniel were less strong.

He said that his parents had helped him pay for the private police academy training. When I asked why law enforcement, he told me that he thought the job would offer variety as well as chances to help people, which he liked to do. This work held genuine appeal for him. He was not interested in his previous work, parking cars. I asked if he had concerns about his personal safety, and his response was that a person either had the mind-set for this work or not—"You can't teach courage," he observed.

> "I was a bit of a zombie—it took away my personality."

We discussed what he recalled about the problems he'd had as a child. "I remember Dr. W. [his first psychiatrist]. I was about six. I had to take the medicine. I didn't understand it. I didn't like it. I felt like I was being put on the spot in terms of what I did. Looking back, I thought of all the medications I had been taking—it now seems odd. One medicine I thought was called 'Koleen' [choline]— it tasted really bad. The Ritalin, I appreciated. It helped me at school. But I was a bit of a zombie—it took away my personality. I remember fourth grade went okay, but then I was at a private Christian school and I got Ds. I didn't like going to the doctor. My friends didn't have to go. Why did I have to see the psychiatrist?

"About two years ago, I got in touch with my birth mom. She told me she was eighteen and my dad was twenty-one [when I was born]. Her name is Michelle and she lives in Colorado. My birth grandmother said she wanted Michelle to keep me and would have helped her take care of me. But it would have been a bad situation, I think. My mom's a bus driver. I also have a half brother; he's seven." When I asked if he was interested in meeting him, he said he would be "someday," but not now.

We speculated on whether the adoption, his behavior, his struggles, and his parents' worries contributed to all the medications he took when he was very young. "You know, I've never gotten a clear answer from my parents. I don't remember that much. I remember the candy machine outside of Dr. W.'s office. That's the kind of thing kids remember."

He reviewed his school performance during the time I was involved with him. "I was at the Christian school in the eighth grade. Things were academically real hard—school was never really my thing. I had only a little bit of trouble in the seventh and eighth grades. I had lots of friends. I was playing lots of soccer. I was on traveling teams."

When I was no longer involved with his care, Daniel went to a large Christian high school and was very involved in sports for about three years. In his junior year, he was kicked out of school for drinking off campus. Trouble and suspensions seemed to follow him. "I was getting into trouble a lot. Probably had a lot of testosterone going. I was confused and angry." During the second half of his junior year, he attended a Christian-oriented private school for young people with learning disabilities and mild behavior problems.

"It felt like a prison, but it was mindless. The work was totally easy." He then rejoined his class at his former high school for his senior year and graduated with them at the end of the year.

In his junior year, he was kicked out of school for drinking off campus.

He went on to talk in more detail about his life. "I stopped Ritalin my sophomore year in high school. I thought I could focus without it, and it took away my personality. I went to community college at Sacramento City College. I wanted to get away from home—it forced me to grow up. But I finished my two years at Diablo Valley College. I was working and going to school. I didn't live at home—I rented an apartment and lived with a friend. Then, when I was at the academy, I lived at home for two months to save money. I tried working for my dad—he owns a commercial door company—but I felt that he and my brother [who also works for him] took advantage of me."

The conversation turned to long-ago family dynamics. He acknowledged the difference in the relationships he had with his parents—the relative alliance he felt with his mother and the distance that seemed to exist between him and his father. "Dad never wanted to listen to me. It's now better because he respects what I did in the academy, but I still feel judged by him." He also never felt close to his older brother, Francis, whom he feels still judges him. I remembered that Francis usually seemed frustrated by his parents' inability to control Daniel.

AN ADMISSION OF PATERNITY

Daniel smiled for the first time forty-five minutes into the interview when he told me about calling his biological grandmother, who was very interested in his life and what he was doing. He then mentioned that two years previously, like his biological parents, he'd fathered a child who was put up for adoption.

"Jenna, my girlfriend, and I were about twenty-two; we were both adopted. Boy, she made it hell for me during the pregnancy. Her parents kicked her out of her house. We were both too young. Jenna kept me in the dark about her plans. We named her [the baby] Olivia, and I signed away my rights as a parent. I don't know who adopted her, but she would be two now." I was struck by his relative lack of affect in telling me this story; he seemed matter-of-fact. He then reflected, "This nature-nurture thing. I guess nature is pretty important, since I repeated what my mother and father did with me."

He then went back to talking about his adoptive father. "I'm still working on my dad and brother. We watch sports together." I mentioned my theory about his parents disagreeing with one another, and that the special relationship he had with his mother may have alienated his father. "I think you're right. That makes sense," he said, and seemed to be comfortable with that explanation.

"I had thought of joining the military after high school, but I had this relationship and didn't want to give it up. Then I took a class in the administration of justice at the community college—that's when I knew what I wanted to do," he told me.

When I asked whether he ever thought of taking medication again, or whether he felt he needed it, he demurred. "The jobs I've had since then . . . I don't really need the medicine for them." To my query about whether he would have changed anything growing up, or done anything differently, he said, "I'd have been more careful in some of the things I did. But without my problems, I may not have handled my academy training as well. I had more experience even though I was one of the youngest."

As we drove back to my office, Daniel seemed more comfortable and settled; my guess was that he rarely spoke to anyone at this level of detail. I suggested that he talk to his dad about the things we'd discussed, and he liked that idea. It's hard just to talk to these young men without wanting to give them some advice or feedback. But I am no longer their doctor.

GOOD FORTUNE OR GOOD GENES?

I was struck by the contrast between the choices and outcomes of Daniel and Kevin. They both had extremely rocky early childhoods. Daniel's behavior seemed to improve in middle school, but got quite problematic again in high school. And unlike Kevin's parents, Heidi and Frank stayed together, disagreements notwithstanding.

More speculatively, Daniel's parents were not his biological progenitors. Perhaps in this case, that worked in Daniel's favor, in that, temperamentally, Heidi and Frank could be more steady and consistent. They could meet Daniel's own personality needs better than his biological mother and father would have been able to do. As Daniel theorized, it's tempting to make a link between his biological parents' actions—impulsive or otherwise—in conceiving Daniel and Daniel's own early paternity. Barkley's data certainly indicate higher rates of unwed fathers in his long-term cohorts. But it's close to impossible to separate the effects of nature versus nurture in events as complex as making babies out of wedlock, or divorce.

Both Kevin and Daniel gravitated to occupations (military and police work) that have highly structured hierarchies.

It's also interesting that both Kevin and Daniel gravitated to occupations (military and police work) that have highly structured hierarchies, as though both instinctively knew they needed that kind of environment to operate successfully. It's too soon to say how Daniel will do as a police officer. Yet it is well known that police officers and felons often come from the same socioeconomic group and neighborhoods. I don't believe anyone has done research into the question of whether there are higher rates of ADHD in the childhoods of those who join the police, or whether police would be in Barkley's H– adult categories (his group of former patients who as adults no longer exhibit ADHD problem behaviors). But I wouldn't be that surprised to find out they are.

> I don't believe anyone has done research into the question of whether there are higher rates of ADHD in the childhoods of those who join the police.

Bad outcomes raise questions about the role of nature and nurture in children's development. The discussion quickly becomes more dramatic and takes on social and political implications. If it's really "all in the genes" and wiring, why spend a great deal of time and money to change a child's environments via parenting, education, and so forth? Early identification and treatment with medication logically follows, or so goes the argument in some circles.

However, the answer to how to prevent the problems of crime, violence, or young unwed parenthood will not come from better diagnoses or earlier interventions. Yes, an individual child may be helped. But to focus our energies on the individual is to divert our attention and energies (that is, money and funding) from the broader socioeconomic, political, and public health issues of indigent families. I'm not sure how we can change the environments and living situations of children and families who don't have the resources to address the comorbidities that may become, in the end, the serious life problems of those with ADHD.

8

. . .

The Dissatisfieds
Medication and Self-Medication

Jim Hassler, whom I featured in *Running on Ritalin*, was a nearly sixteen-year-old discontented adolescent when I first met him in July 1991. Here's an excerpt on him:

> *His parents were strong (and early) believers in the chemical-imbalance theory of behavior. Jim wasn't underperforming at all. He was clearly both bright and hardworking; he was getting straight As in high school. Even off medication, Jim earned excellent grades. But he was very clear about how much harder it was for him to concentrate and stay at the top of his class without Ritalin.*

In addition to a possible attention deficit, Jim seemed to exhibit anxious and obsessional qualities; his parents, both with postdoctoral degrees, appeared to be equally driven. Though his parents did not notice any difference in Jim's performance on or off the drug, they

He was very clear about how much harder it was for him to concentrate and stay at the top of his class without Ritalin.

supported and respected his wish to continue taking it.

I was uncomfortable, however—I never felt that I was treating an illness (ADD). Eventually, in the running for valedictorian of his high school class, Jim himself became dissatisfied with Ritalin, saying it made him less sociable. More to the point, it didn't address what he and I came to call his "existential angst"—never feeling quite happy or contented with himself. So Jim and I embarked on a grand tour of psychotropic drugs used to treat ADD, depression, and anxiety disorders; we went through several SSRIs (the Prozac family), desipramine, Welbutrin, and BuSpar, among others. Typically, Jim would report that the newest drug was finally "the one," but within a few months, he would complain that he wasn't feeling right.

While in college, Jim did his share of self-medicating with alcohol, marijuana, cocaine, and the occasional hallucinogen. He had some difficult times—during a particularly low point while a freshman in college, he contemplated suicide. With some help, he pulled out of it and graduated with a 4.0 average.

Jim's quest for the perfect medication eventually led him to the Hallowell Center in Massachusetts, a mecca for ADD sufferers. He returned with a new drug (for him)—nortriptyline (Pamelor)—considered by the psychiatric cognoscenti (circa 1996) to be effective for his type of generalized angst. As usual, he hailed the new medication as a breakthrough.

My private clinical notes take Jim's story a bit further. By 1998, he had given Dexedrine (a Ritalin variant) another try, but said it left him feeling "obsessed." At the time, he was working in real estate and living in New York with a man. (At seventeen, Jim had announced he was gay, first to me and then to his parents, who had suspected it for a year or two.) He told me he was trying St. John's wort, but might restart the nortriptyline again.

My last note is from September 2004: "Phone call from NY—inquiring about his new diagnosis of bipolar, wondering if that was missed when I knew him." And that was the last I heard from Jim until I found him in late 2009.

Of all my interviewees, he was the only one who was initially reluctant to speak with me. He was slow in replying to my first email, and when I finally phoned to ask about his reservations, he told me that he had been unhappy with what I had written about him in *Running on Ritalin*. When I offered him the opportunity to review what I wrote about him for this book, he agreed to see me.

Because I wanted to speak with him face-to-face as I had done with my other now-adult former patients, I flew to New York and met him not far from where he lived on Manhattan's Lower East Side, a fashionable neighborhood within blocks of where, ninety years ago, my Jewish relatives from Poland had grown up. I was a bit early but still fretted when he didn't arrive exactly on time. Had he forgotten? Maybe he had changed his mind at the last minute. But then I saw a tall, thin man with a fashionable haircut waving his hand above his head to catch my eye and greet me. We shook hands warmly on the street.

We met in a delightful replica of a French bistro and bar that was just opening up for the day; we were the first to sit down, so it was completely quiet. Jim's speech and mannerisms still had the mildly affected dramatic style I remembered from thirteen years ago. Though he was fashionably dressed, he later told me he was broke. He was also quite hungry, and I wondered if he had been eating well. At thirty-four, he was as thin as he had been at twenty-one, the last time I'd seen him.

The previous evening, I had reread the section of *Running on*

Ritalin that concerned him, but was still uncertain about what he had found to be upsetting. Because I wanted to get the subject out of the way early, I asked him. "You know, Dr. Diller," he said, "I just felt some things were not accurate. You changed some things. I'm not reluctant to talk to you now, even if you have a different opinion from me. I just want you to get it right—I mean, for the general public. I think it was something about substance abuse."

I had written that Jim had used illegal drugs, but perhaps I had gotten it wrong, or had overestimated his use. However, I had disguised his identity, and no one except he and his family would have been able to recognize him from my discussion. To clear the air, I asked him to start from the beginning, before he met me, and describe his experiences with doctors and medication.

"I started out very young—I think I was about five or possibly a little older—when we lived in New Orleans. Then we moved to California and I started Dexedrine, then switched to Adderall. I had another MD in Orinda before you. In college, I started antidepressants," he summarized.

A RACE TO NOWHERE

Even with his superb grades, he didn't get into his first-choice colleges, Stanford and the Ivy League schools. "I felt I had failed in not going to the schools my mother had wanted me to go to. At the same time, I've had this elitist streak of my own that wasn't satisfied." He wound up attending the University of California, Berkeley, which many consider to be the best public university in the country.

"What about freshman year at Cal?" I asked. "I recall that you got very depressed. On a scale of zero to ten—zero being the worst and ten the best— how lousy did you feel during your freshman year?"

"Oh, about zero to two. You know, I've been at zero to two a couple of times since then also." He borrowed my pen and drew a graph on one of the paper placemats; the vertical axis had zero at the bottom and ten at the top. Then he drew a line along the horizontal axis, which represented his mood over time. The line never hit higher than five, and dipped to nearly zero at three points. "This is my life," he said. He pointed to one of the dips. "This was when I first moved to New York in about 2000. I was very low."

I reminded him of the time he told me that he'd "looked long and hard at a razor blade," and he replied that, though he'd done many self-destructive things, he would never attempt suicide. "Philosophically, I'm not opposed to it, but I've always felt I had choices. I've never come down to doing it, but I've thought about it constantly."

Returning to our discussion of his earlier life, he said that after he graduated, he lived in San Francisco for a year before going to New York. "New York was wonderful. I was not happy with the people in San Francisco. Also, compared to New York, San Francisco was boring."

His comment about San Francisco being boring recalled another term he'd used years ago, and I asked him to explain it. "Jim, tell me about this 'dysthymia' thing. It's your expression. You used it years ago with me. What did you mean by it?"

"Dysthymia—I don't know the difference between it and depression. Throughout my whole life, little has given me pleasure. Things that people like don't do anything for me. I just don't get what they're getting. I go to beautiful places with my family. My mother says, 'Why don't you like it?' I say, 'I think it's okay, but no big deal.'

"Dysthymia . . . Throughout my whole life, little has given me pleasure."

"My life is not good, but I'm reasonably content at the moment. I've come very far; I have complaints, but I'm not unhappy or miserable at home." He points to the graph on the placemat. "I'm actually above midline at the moment. Not that much, but okay. I don't believe people can be great all the time. That's actually mania." I recalled how Jim had always sprinkled his conversation with psychiatric diagnostic jargon.

When I asked him what he liked about New York, he said it was its energy and access. "You never have to leave. Everything is at the tip of your fingers. There are interesting people—more my type."

He continued his saga. "When I got here, I didn't work for a long time, maybe a year and a half. My first job was with an Internet company that went bust in 2001 [during the dot-com meltdown]. Then I got a job at a law firm as an administrator-type person. I was not a lawyer but I felt smarter than most of them. Yet they were making way more money than I was."

In this comment, I recognized a recurrent theme from Jim's past: his feeling that he is intellectually and culturally superior to his peers but is not sufficiently recognized or appreciated. I've always felt this to be part of what he calls his "dysthymia," or generalized unhappiness.

He continued, "But really, I wanted to go to Europe, so I chose a famous business school in Barcelona. Most people here haven't heard of it, but it's quite well known in Europe; it was ranked a number one school by the *Wall Street Journal*. I was there two years."

Our discussion then drifted back to Jim's experiences with psychiatric drugs.

"I tried Lamictal. It helped initially, but then I felt the same things. I started lithium in 2005, when I was thirty; it's the only drug that's never gone down—it's only gone up. It's the best thing that's happened to me."

Lamictal (approved for use with epilepsy) and lithium are employed in the treatment of bipolar disorder, the label for what used to be called manic depression. By Jim's own account, he never demonstrated true mania—behaviors that include grandiose ideation (thinking you're Napoleon), enormous energy (staying awake for days on end), or other extremely erratic acts (making thousands of dollars' worth of credit card purchases in a short period of time). However, Jim clearly felt that lithium was quite helpful in improving the lows of his moods.

While it is conceivable that there are doctors who would categorize Jim's life course as consistent with bipolar disorder, as a more strict diagnostician, I would shrug off this diagnostic conundrum and simply consider lithium as yet another drug for Jim to try in his search for emotional satisfaction and stability.

Many find lithium's side effects difficult to take, and I asked him how he handled them. "I have a very small tremor. It doesn't bother me. Even if I knew I was going to die from this drug in two years—well, maybe not two—I would still take it." He also mentioned that he took a medication to counteract the drug's effect on his thyroid.

We then moved on to talk about how he makes his medication decisions. "I'm like a psychiatry machine. I read. I study. It's my own tenacity. I pushed my doctor to get the lithium. But it's now been five and a half years. There's been none of the real lows since then. I take 1,500 milligrams—two in the morning and three at night. The time-released kind. The psychiatrist has been hands-off. I upped my own lithium. That was good. I could order my own lithium in Spain. I told my doctor my dose and he accepted it."

> "I'm like a psychiatry machine. I read. I study. It's my own tenacity. I pushed my doctor to get the lithium."

His comment about Spain led to another example of Jim's perpetual discontent. "I loved Europe. I never wanted to come back. I hated Bush. But I was still depressed. Not badly, but it just wasn't right. It was also difficult job-wise, so in 2007, I came back to the U.S. I still have problems in my life—I'm still only at 90 percent. But for me, that's reasonably content.

"But the job situation here . . . as they would say in Spain, it's *'fatale.'* Now I'm working in real estate; I make about a thousand dollars a month. I'm on Medicaid and food stamps. My parents still help me and I'm thirty-four. I'm working at a high-end agency, but I don't have the will to do it. It's the damn dysthymia, but I'm so much happier than I was.

"The Medicaid doctors are very careful with me. So this is my situation. I just started taking Adderall again, 2.5 milligrams, and it works! I get so many things done. But if I take it two days in a row, I get anxious, so I only take it as I need it. Then, there's the Lamictal; I take 100 or 125 milligrams. And the lithium. I also occasionally take Ambien [for sleep]."

Okay, I thought, *those are the legal drugs,* but I also knew Jim had tried many illegal drugs in the past to try to cure his blues. So I asked him about his history with that category of pharmaceuticals.

"I love pot but the rest I hate. Oh, I'll have a drink about once a month. Marijuana much more. Cocaine, I just tried it. I hated it— it's like Adderall. I tried Ecstasy; it made me anxious but I felt good. Oh, and I liked mushrooms. Actually, do you know about Salvia [*Salvia divinorum,* a psychoactive plant that can induce "out of body" experiences]? I like that, too. Now, I'm just using weed occasionally."

Jim had always struck me as something of a pharmaceutical "groupie" rather than a drug abuser, so this list didn't surprise me.

From drugs to lifestyle—Jim and his family had lived in Orinda; like its neighbor, Walnut Creek, it's a bastion of middle- to upper-middle-class conservative values. I asked him when he had realized he was gay.

"I was in the closet when I met you—I was conflicted. But you moved me in a direction that was helpful." He went on to say that it soon became a nonissue for him. "Other things made the gay thing worse. I had this constant depression, different degrees of it." When I reminded him about how alienated he'd seemed to feel from his Orinda peers, he concurred. "You're right. Looking back, Orinda was not the most tolerant place, but my depression was the biggest thing."

At the time of our interview, Jim was in a relationship with a man named Peter, and had been for a year and a half. "That's the longest relationship for me. He's German, a highly functional private banker for the richest people in the world. But he has health problems, psychological stuff . . . social anxiety, stomachaches.

"There's no passion anymore, no sex in our relationship. We each have different places. I still love him; I've been thinking about breaking up. He's a good person. I really didn't have any relationships before Peter—I had flings. But since starting lithium, I'm 'born again'; it's like my religion."

> "Since starting lithium, I'm 'born again'; it's like my religion."

Jim brought me up-to-date on his biological family. "Dad retired five years ago [from his position as dean of an Eastern law college]. He'd been depressed. You know, my father was always the mother for me—he was the nurturer. My mother and I had significant problems. We would fight whenever we spoke. How often I'd end up screaming at her! But by the way, she's happy." I knew she had been taking antidepressants herself in the 1990s.

We speculated about the role his mother's criticisms and judgments played in the development of his own chronic unhappiness and self-criticism—nothing is good enough, he is not good enough—but ultimately, he dismissed it. "I think it's biological. My dad is suffering the same way, only less so. I've been telling him to get on lithium like me."

Jim's brother, Jack, younger by two years, had become an attorney. The two weren't very close. "Jack's detached. I see him once every year or two. We lead very different lives. My brother is also bright. I was the one who always did better in school. Yet he's a lawyer—and I'm on food stamps."

I asked him, "What about psychotherapy? Did you find it of any value?"

"Psychotherapy? I'm not impressed with it. These people may be good or even spectacular, but I'm not impressed that they've done that much with me."

As our interview wound down, Jim mentioned that he had a few questions for me. I assumed he wanted to know about me and what I was doing these days, but he was still searching for the drug answer to his discontent. "With lithium, I'm happy to live, but I don't have passion. I'm thinking of Abilify or TMS."

Thirteen years later, he's still looking for a drug answer from me and I'm still trying to do therapy with him.

I told him that Abilify is the latest "new kid on the block" drug, a lot like Risderdal or Zyprexa, without as much weight gain. On the TMS—transcranial magnetic stimulation—I told him I didn't think much of it, but I suspected he'd want to try that, too. My advice to him was to think about what he wanted to do, not what he should do. Thirteen years later, he's still looking for a drug answer from me and I'm still trying to do therapy with him.

Soon after, we left the restaurant. He accompanied me a couple of blocks to my next appointment, then we shook hands and said good-bye.

RITALIN AS A GATEWAY DRUG OR PROTECTOR

Since the mid-1990s, for both children and adults, evaluations for ADHD and ADD have become the diagnostic ticket of admission for a whole host of emotional and performance problems. Jim was a harbinger of this trend. I cannot say that ADD was ever his primary problem, even though he has taken prescription stimulants such as Dexedrine and Adderall intermittently—to perhaps some benefit—since the age of seven.

But especially with adults, it's often very hard to distinguish the true underperformance of ADD from the dissatisfaction of having very high standards. Jim was continually dissatisfied. Was this a permanent biological state, or was it a result of how he was raised? Probably a bit of both. His parents no doubt played a role, but they were very hard on themselves, too. Was it in their genes or the way they themselves had been raised—how far back do we go? Jim's father had a very successful career, and his mother was quite bright. I've wondered whether her depression and irritability, as Jim put it, was to some extent a cultural artifact—she seemed to have just missed out on the career opportunities the feminist revolution afforded.

It seems a shame, though, that Jim hadn't changed much in the eighteen years I'd known him. It's conceivable that his sense of failure career-wise had some self-fulfilling aspects, affecting his motivation and leading to underperformance to the point that, at age thirty-four, he was on Medicaid and food stamps. Obviously, he was capable—he'd earned a degree from UC Berkeley and an MBA in Barcelona—but his successes were not sustained. During our lunchtime conversation, I had suggested that he consider volunteer work, because I had a hunch that Jim believed that working as a lawyer or businessman was fundamentally not "worthwhile," even though one could make a lot of money. But then, not making money also made him feel unworthy . . . and on it goes.

Jim's search for happiness led him to try countless legal and illegal drugs. While marijuana was his primary illicit drug of choice, Jim generally depended on pharmaceuticals. However, many believe that most substance abusers have a biologically based problem and are simply self-medicating to either improve or numb themselves.

The rates of substance abuse in Barkley's Milwaukee cohort of adult ADHD children were quite high; nearly one-quarter of those in the H+ group (who still met the criteria for ADHD as adults) admitted to alcohol and/or drug abuse. Not surprisingly, children who additionally met criteria for conduct disorder (CD) were at the highest risk of abusing substances.

Curiously, for alcohol, this rate just missed being significantly higher than the community controls; people from the lower- to lower-middle-class environments from which Barkley obtained his clinical and control samples had higher rates of substance abuse as well as more antisocial activity than my middle- to upper-middle-class cohort. Compared to my group, this class difference led to poorer long-term outcomes for those in both Barkley's ADHD and community control groups.

While I did not always specifically ask the young adults I interviewed for this book about their alcohol and drug use, it came up regularly in our conversations. Though virtually all of them had used illegal drugs and drank alcohol, none spoke of these substances as central to their current lives. I wonder again whether the supports and interventions they received growing up spared them the worst aspects of alcohol and drug abuse.

Since Ritalin is a stimulant much like methamphetamine and cocaine, parents have always worried about "addicting" their children with Ritalin.

Public controversy continues over whether taking Ritalin as a child sensitizes or predisposes children toward future drug abuse as adults. Since Ritalin is a stimulant much like methamphetamine and cocaine, parents have always worried about "addicting" their children with Ritalin. There is some evidence from animal and adult volunteer studies that even small doses of Ritalin change the body's autonomic nervous system (such as eye blink and heart rate) to conform more closely to a drug abuser's patterns. However, some experts have said that it's just the opposite—that a child taking Ritalin for ADHD is *protected* against future drug abuse.

When given the opportunity to press a lever for food or an amphetamine, animals exposed to a single high dose of the drug given intravenously will become addicted (select the drug more and more) quicker than those unexposed to the drug. Rats will actually starve to death if allowed to choose between amphetamines and food. However, while these basic research findings are of concern, they have not been universally proven to hold true for children. Only one prospective study, undertaken by UC Berkeley researcher Nadine Lambert, showed an increase in rates of cocaine and cigarette use by young adults who, as children, were given Ritalin-type drugs for ADHD. She compared the treated group to ADHD children who weren't given the medication.

Lambert said that she wasn't looking for this finding when she began her life's work of following four hundred children for two decades. She initiated her project because she was interested in learning whether or not special education interventions made long-term differences for ADHD children. Her discovery about the increased use of cocaine and cigarettes was accidental.

Regardless, she felt her findings had to be reported, and did so at a famous "Consensus Conference" on ADHD and Ritalin sponsored by the National Institutes of Health in Washington, D.C., in 1998. I remember it well because I was there and observed the reactions of both the press and the other academics in the conference hall. After Lambert's presentation, the reporters rushed to their keyboards, and the next morning, the idea that "Ritalin causes drug abuse" was trumpeted in newspaper headlines and on television. Meanwhile, researchers in the audience were baffled and angry in equal measure; they thought Lambert must be wrong with her data or methods, and that she was frightening the public unnecessarily.

As it turned out, her methodology left her open to criticism. She hadn't randomized who in her cohort received or didn't receive medication; the families themselves got to choose whether or not their children were given the drug. Critics said her results may have been corrupted by the "medication bias" effect—the families choosing to medicate their children may have had worse problems, which later led to higher rates of addiction. In her defense, Lambert had done her best to match both groups of ADHD kids; all were judged to be quite similar at the start of her study in the 1970s. It wasn't until the 1990s that state-of-the-art studies required randomization—families entering a study aren't given a choice, but rather are randomly assigned to respective groups.

Other researchers rushed to publish studies that contradicted Lambert's results, and she spent the rest of her life—which ended in 2006 in an automobile accident—trying to defend her study. The Harvard Pediatric Psychopharmacology Clinic (Joseph Biederman's group) quickly published an analysis of a small sample of patients for whom they said Ritalin demonstrated a "protective" effect—kids who had used Ritalin were abusing less as adults. But a close read of

Prior Ritalin use neither sensitized them to nor protected them from future drug abuse.

the families in this study raised other questions about its conclusion. Families who chose not to medicate their kids had higher rates of substance abuse themselves—certainly a potential confounding factor (a risk factor that affects the results of a study) for their children's future abuse.

Fortunately, Barkley had enough ADHD children in his follow-up cohorts who never received medication to get a better read on the sensitization-protection controversy. His findings showed that prior Ritalin use neither sensitized them to nor protected them from future drug abuse. His results seemed closer to my experience. Family and neighborhood (which are causally implicated in ODD-CD problems) play a larger role in future potential drug abuse than whether or not the child has taken Ritalin. In my group of patients, the families' higher socioeconomic status and the interventions they brought to bear for their children seemed to have a protective effect overall.

However, the bigger Ritalin drug abuse problem for our society today is not the cumulative effects of prior Ritalin use in children, but rather the growing use and abuse of illegally obtained prescription stimulants, particularly among older teens and college students.

ADDERALL MAKES THE COLLEGE SCENE

This isn't an entirely new story; underground abuse of amphetamines has been documented since their synthesis in 1929. Following World War II, GIs who were given amphetamines by their officers during combat continued to use and abuse the drug once they returned home. During the mid- to late 1960s, counterculture hippies turned to legal amphetamines and

Today's abuser is most likely an affluent older teen or college student.

Ritalin, with devastating results—by 1969, graffiti warning that "Speed Kills" began appearing in San Francisco's Haight-Ashbury district. Finally, the grandmothers of today's young abusers may recall that during the 1970s, many women became addicted to the Dexedrine prescribed by their doctors as a weight loss drug.

Short-acting Adderall is a favorite because it can be easily crushed and snorted.

Today's abuser is most likely an affluent older teen or college student. After alcohol, prescription drugs now top marijuana as the second-most-likely abused substance. Opiates like Oxycontin are the number one choice, followed by drugs for ADHD and ADD. Short-acting Adderall is a favorite because it can be easily crushed and snorted (and more rarely liquefied and used intravenously).

College students also like Adderall because it has a relatively short duration—about four hours. When students are asked about their use of pharmaceuticals, "power studying" and cramming appear to be the most common reasons they're taken, though "getting high" is also frequently cited. On some campuses, up to 35 percent of the student body has admitted to the illegal use of a prescription stimulant. On a *60 Minutes* investigation aired in April 2010, a college counselor at the University of Kentucky (the campus with the highest published rate) felt that, by senior year, rates of abuse were as high as 80 percent among the fraternity-sorority subpopulation at the school.

Virtually all students know where the pills can be obtained cheaply and quickly—most commonly from students who have legal prescriptions from their doctors. Some of these prescriptions aren't too difficult to obtain. Near some campuses, there are reportedly medical offices that rather easily dispense both the ADHD diagnosis and prescriptions to treat it.

The illegal use of amphetamine-type drugs for people without

ADHD or ADD has become so widespread that an ethical case for using the pills to enhance cognitive abilities has been made by prominent researchers in prestigious journals such as *Nature*. It doesn't matter that these drugs really do not improve mental performance or complex cognition—what they *do* improve is the ability to stick with boring, difficult, or repetitive tasks.

But more importantly, those attempting to justify the use of amphetamines for everyone ignore the risk of abuse and addiction. In the only survey of the general population that I'm aware of, researchers found that in the age group of fifteen to twenty-five, one in ten illegal users of prescription stimulants went on to develop use consistent with abuse and addiction. "One in ten" means that nine out of ten appear to be able to use the drugs with relative safety.

In 2002 when the survey was performed, about 750,000 young people had tried prescription stimulants illegally. However, as the number of casual users has undoubtedly grown into the millions, the 10 percent who struggle with the drugs represent countless individual tragedies and a major societal problem. Anyone who has studied the history of these drugs will conclude the same historical inevitability.

Oddly enough, Ritalin is safer for children than it is for adults. Children neither have free access to the drug nor do they like higher dosages, which most say make them feel "nervous" and "weird." Older teens and adults do have access, and many actually enjoy higher dosages or the unconventional delivery methods previously mentioned. They say they feel "powerful" and "grand."

In short, prescription stimulant abuse is the growing, threatening specter behind the broadened ADHD/ADD diagnosis and its treatment with Ritalin-type drugs. Again, if history is our guide, there will eventually be too many casualties (especially among the prominent, wealthy, and powerful). At that point, a backlash against the drugs, especially to treat adult ADHD, will result. But until then, my experience and cynicism suggest that there are too many groups (including doctors and drug companies) making money in this process and that the demand is too great for any effective reform or control to take place before I retire at some point in the next fifteen years. Anyone who knows about the Trojan Wars will appreciate how much like Cassandra (she was given the gift of prophesy but the curse that no one would believe her) I have felt when talking about this issue.

ADHD: SALVATION OR CRUTCH

Katie wasn't in *Running on Ritalin*, but I immediately thought of her when contemplating which of my former patients I should include in this book. Katie was seventeen when I met her in 1996, and I was reminded of her in 2007, when a reporter for the *Los Angeles Times* called to ask if I knew any teenagers who had taken Ritalin in the mid-1990s and now were in their late twenties. I tracked down Katie and asked if she'd be willing to be interviewed by the reporter. She agreed, and I later read about her in a larger feature story that appeared in 2008.

Initially, I planned to convey Katie's story as part of Chapter 4, which featured Jenny, Lauren, and Jennifer. But once I met with her, I knew she fit best in this chapter on the dissatisfied and discontented. Her experiences with using and abusing Ritalin also illustrate, on a much more personal level, the societal fears and concerns mentioned earlier in this chapter.

Here are some chart notes on Katie from 1996:

Looks at papers and clocks while we are talking. Trouble at school, trouble with organization since seventh grade. Attending a premier private boarding school in the Bay Area. "I can't make myself do it

[schoolwork]. I procrastinate until mid-term." A in English, Cs in
math and chemistry. Before puberty (according to parents) exuber-
ant and unsettled. Could focus well on projects in earlier grades.
Became more restless in puberty and after.

The school reported that Katie was a nervous kid—adrift, lacking concentration, and running quickly through boyfriends and
projects. They also mentioned that she was easily fascinated with
new subjects but was equally quick to drop them. The report closed
with a provocative insight: "Driven, but rarely happy."

In private, Katie told me that she relied heavily on medications,
including antacids, pain relievers, and herbal remedies, but also used
hallucinogens about once a month. I suggested a medication trial,
and she was willing, as were her parents. Ritalin improved her school
performance and made her studying more efficient; during the next
year, her senior year in high school, Katie seemed happier and was
preparing to apply to East Coast colleges. My last note on Katie is
from August 1998, after her freshman year at Sarah Lawrence:

*Katie had a successful year . . . and is planning to return for her
sophomore year. Did quite well academically and will try no medication after the first month upon her return. In general, she appears happy, physically looks good, and her attitude about life
appears greatly improved.*

Now, thirteen years later, I was going to see her again. She
taught art and set up gallery shows, and had a busy schedule—in
fact, she'd already canceled on me twice. But the second time, I was
able to pin her down for lunch on a Sunday in San Francisco. She
chose a place across the street from the San Francisco Art Institute,
where she now taught a class.

I arrived first and chose to sit outside on the patio in the sun. As the appointed time approached, I began to worry that perhaps she wasn't going to show, but at five minutes after the hour, Katie came out to the patio. I had also been concerned that I might not recognize her, but when I saw her, I knew her immediately. Now thirty-one, she was about five foot seven, with brown hair pulled up tightly. She wore a fashionable pantsuit and attractive drop earrings. I noticed tiny pockmarks, or scars, on her cheeks, which I thought may have been due to acne. (Later, I learned the actual cause of these slight disfigurations.) I spied a small tattoo on the inside of her right wrist. All in all, she looked like the aspiring young artist I believed her to be.

Unlike anyone else I interviewed for this book, Katie immediately began with her own series of questions for me. She seemed quite interested in the book project and the details of the outcomes of the young adults I had already interviewed (she was the last). I was so caught up in my own excitement about it and in seeing her that I forgot a cardinal rule of the psychiatric interview: Before you answer a question, ask one. So I pulled back and said, "Katie, why are you so interested in these stories?"

As I later realized, she only half answered me. "I've gone back and forth between believing that ADHD and ADD really exist or that they don't. Somehow, I feel ADHD is real and ADD isn't." I accepted her answer and didn't pursue it any further. Not until the very end of our nearly two hours together did I learn the full reason for her continuing interest in the diagnosis. But her answers provided an easy segue to the central question of the book: how the kids, now grown up, feel about having taking Ritalin.

AN ARTIST'S JOURNEY

She had clearly given this some thought. "The medicine helped me a lot. But it also had to do with how our educational system is set up. You see, we are basically animals who follow our own interests. I could work in the photography darkroom for six hours, but I could never focus on the academics. I wanted to do well. My teachers were great, but my brain would just run. I had an extreme turnaround with my grades on Ritalin. I'm not sure how it affected my math skills, since I didn't have to take math anymore by the time I started the medication. With the medicine, I was able to focus outside my areas of interest, which were art and photography."

I asked her to tell me a bit about her history before she met me. She had gotten into trouble while at a conservative prep school in Southern California; at that point, her family transferred her to the Bay Area prep school she was attending when we met. She had a good opinion of the school and some of the teachers, but said she still had a hard time concentrating on schoolwork unless it involved creative writing or reading. She went on to say that she had maintained contact with her former philosophy teacher, a Mr. S. "He really knew me," she said.

Coincidentally, it was Mr. S. whom I had contacted for Katie's evaluation, and during the interview, I read her his comments. She was intrigued. "It's interesting that he picked up on these things. I had a lot of anxiety, and put more on myself. My mom wanted me to go see someone. I didn't accept that I was unhappy.

"I was always a troublemaker—I would question authority. But when I applied to schools like Sarah Lawrence and Mills, I got in. Why did I pick Sarah Lawrence? I decided be-

> "I was always a troublemaker—I would question authority."

forehand, before I ever saw the school. This is where my impulsivity comes in. I didn't do any research. I had already gone to boarding school, so the first year of college wasn't too hard. Sarah Lawrence was good; they had an open curriculum and there weren't a lot of requirements. But there were only three classes per semester, and if they were bad, then you were stuck. I randomly filled all my requirements freshman year—and there was no math requirement! Later, I regretted not going to an art school. Maybe then I would have had better teachers to prepare me for the art world.

"I did my junior year [of college] in Madrid. When I lived in Madrid, I had a Spanish boyfriend and we stayed together through my senior year. I was [generally] planning to go back to Europe after graduating but I had no specific plan. Instead, I went back to the family winery. Eduardo, my boyfriend, came for three months, and it was hell. But I was stubborn, so we stuck it out. Then he left as scheduled and I was supposed to follow."

However, instead of going back to Spain, she relocated to New York and lived in Brooklyn. She had inherited money from her uncle and was old enough to have access to it, so she didn't have to worry about supporting herself through work. Nonetheless, she said that for her own self-esteem, she felt that she needed to have a job. "I had too much guilt and anxiety if I didn't work at all," she observed.

"I'd take photos and work on my portfolio, but I really didn't know what I was doing. It always weighed heavily on me. If I could just accept it [the fact of having money], it would have been fine. But I'd make myself go home instead of staying out all night, just to act responsibly. I did do a few little jobs, but having the money was a big-time negative incentive to work.

"Was it ADD, or was it that I was never forced to do anything as a child?"

"In Spain, I had gotten into the clubbing scene, the looks . . . I did that for a while in New York, too. I'd go shopping too much. I had a lot of self-hatred and self-criticism. I'm not hating myself as much these days. Was it ADD, or was it that I was never forced to do anything as a child?" she mused out loud.

I still hadn't realized how much Katie was struggling to understand the relative effects of biological versus learned experience on her self-image and present state. Later, it all made sense to me. But I shared my interpretation with her: that her persistence and stubbornness as a child—combined with her parents' reluctance and inability to really control her—might have had something to do with her self-control issues.

She recalled her childhood. "They didn't spoil us. It wasn't fancy. We lived nine miles outside of town. No television. My sister was three years younger. She's a bookworm, an academic. I was the rowdy tomboy. I would play out in the woods. They let us pick the schools we wanted to go to."

Then she returned to her memories of living in New York. "I had started interning at a little gallery. Photography was art in college, but in New York, I realized that it would have to be commercial—it couldn't just be fun. I saw how it was to work with big fashion photographers and I wasn't ready to do that. I also started taking classes at the International Center of Photography." After that, she applied to the San Francisco Art Institute (SFAI) because she wanted to move back to the Bay Area. Once there, she earned an MFA in two years, but by the time she graduated, she hadn't figured out what she wanted to do for a career. It was apparently a rather tumultuous period for her.

"My boyfriend, Dean, was from New York City. We were together for five years. He moved out here with me, but he has his own place. I prefer my own place. Then I started having a thing with a guy at school. Both relationships broke up during the end of my first year at SFAI. It's tough when your art is self-portraiture and you have a bad time with boyfriends—your art makes you look bad, too. Then I met Colton. He and I got together my second year at SFAI, and we're still together.

"I applied for a job as a junior lecturer at SFAI and teach the undergrad class—the first class students take; unfortunately, I've had some coteaching issues. I also teach photography at a free after-school art class for high school students in San Francisco. I love the students, but struggle with the bosses there, too. I recently had a show, plus I work for my family, building a new website and selling their produce at farmers' markets."

For a thirty-one-year-old artist, she seemed quite accomplished. Two jobs, one show—not bad for the art scene, since it seems that most artists have to take day jobs as waiters or waitresses to survive.

RITALIN—THE SEDUCER, THE DESTROYER

But she wanted to get back to Ritalin—she had something important she wanted to tell me. "After you, I got it through the school psychiatrist at Sarah Lawrence. He was an old man who was horrible. He was just out of touch; I couldn't talk to him. I took it during my sophomore year. But not in Spain." Assuming I knew why she stopped, I thought "no big deal" and tried to move the conversation on to other matters. She wasn't done, though.

"I started snorting it and got addicted . . . but if you're doing something like that every day, you can't eat, you can't sleep."

"I know exactly when I stopped: the first semester of my sophomore year. And I know why I stopped! I started snorting it and got addicted. I tried it once or twice with friends, and it was fun, but after that, for about a month, I did it alone every day in my room. No one knew, but it was affecting my relationships and I was losing weight. I tried to stop once, and failed. Then I kicked it. I can't remember specifically hitting bottom, but if you're doing something like that every day, you can't eat, you can't sleep—it was the worst insomnia. That's what it was in the end: It was just too physically uncomfortable."

Katie had shared her problem with her friend, Melissa, but hadn't told her parents. She thought they'd feel as though it was their fault. She continued, "I knew I couldn't take it for ADD. That wasn't it. It [ADD] wasn't real. It was cultural. It isn't a real thing. I never had a problem focusing on photography. I took a class, 'Illness and Metaphor,' you know . . . Sontag. I did my project on ADD and interviewed Sarah Lawrence students. I still continued to do well in school. It was a good environment for someone with ADD tendencies. I went to the polar opposite on how I felt about it [ADD].

"I do still have a hard time focusing on the mundane and the repetitive. I can't keep things clean to save my life. I listen to books on tape or a podcast when I clean, and I can do the dishes—there's a beginning and an end to those tasks. But bills don't have a beginning or end. I have no system for where to put them. I've had things turned off—not the electricity, but the phone, yes.

"I got really depressed last year around my birthday. I had turned thirty and was taking stock. I didn't want another ten years to just 'go by.' I'm hard on myself and get anxious. I didn't have real depression, but I was an insomniac. I've been going to therapy for years, since puberty, hating myself, being so self-critical. So I had a bit of a breakdown last year, and my therapist and I considered

> **"I got really depressed last year around my birthday. . . . I didn't want another ten years to just 'go by.'"**

medication. I went to a psychiatrist and got a prescription for Pristiq [a new antidepressant]; I've been taking it for a year. It's hard for me to quantify if it's doing any good. But the self-critical part of me has eased; I look at myself more kindly, more rationally."

At this point, there was a very long silence in our conversation. As I waited, I wondered what she was thinking. It seemed as though she was trying to decide whether or not she was going to tell me something. Then she sighed. "Remembering Ritalin . . . I don't know. I really don't know."

Again she paused. "I'm still figuring it out—I don't know how I feel about it. There were so many years I was against it. I don't want to open another can of beans." Her body shifted, and I sensed that she had made her decision. She was going to tell me.

"I restarted ADD medicine six months ago—first Adderall, but it was too strong, too druggy. Then I tried Ritalin, but it was too short term. Now I'm taking Adderall again, but only 10 milligrams twice a day. I haven't come to terms with it. I feel like I need something to help me do what I can't do with pure motivation or desire alone. But I don't know if it's working. Maybe I just changed my expectations. I pick my face really badly [those were the small scars I noticed on her cheeks]. I say to myself, 'Don't do that,' but I still do it. Maybe I just need behavioral modification. Also, I don't want Colton doing too much [work]. He already helps some—he's supportive. He probably thinks I need it. I don't know . . ." Her voice trailed off.

> "I restarted ADD medicine six months ago."

The afternoon had cooled down and we had been talking for nearly two hours. As we walked to our cars, we were still discussing ADD and its medications. "Do you know who *really* has ADD?" was the last thing she asked me.

•   •   •

Katie's story greatly affected me. She was so thoughtful, so articulate, so confused. I appreciated her candor, especially about her abuse of Ritalin in college, and could understand how she could be ambivalent about restarting a stimulant drug. In the end, I think I finally understood why it was so important to her to know if I thought ADD actually existed and who actually *had* it. For Katie and so many others, if ADD truly exists, then what she perceived as personal failures were not entirely her (or her parents') fault. Also, if ADD truly exists, risking her health by taking a drug to treat the condition or disease makes a lot more sense. If it doesn't exist, then perhaps she's just using it as a crutch for her moral or emotional weaknesses and setting herself up to abuse it again.

I wish I could have given Katie a straight black-and-white answer to her question. But for nearly every child or adult struggling with issues of performance and/or impulsivity, the answers are not black and white. Honestly, I'm not certain that even if I had said, "Yes, ADD is a real disease and your use of the medication is like taking insulin for diabetes"—an analogy frequently employed by disease/drug advocates—that answer would have satisfied or addressed Katie's long-term issues of self-doubt and self-criticism.

> If ADD truly exists, then what she perceived as personal failures were not entirely her (or her parents') fault.

Like Jim and some of the other young adults I interviewed for this book, Katie had a strain of discontent and dissatisfaction that left her unhappy—wondering what was wrong with her or what more she could do to become "normal." This unhappiness seemed out of proportion, especially in Katie's case, to the clear successes in her field that she'd achieved at a relatively young age.

In my opinion, whether inborn or learned, this discontent is at the core of the unhappiness that Jim, Katie, and many others who seek the solution of an ADD diagnosis feel. I'm not sure the legal and illegal drugs that treat their ADD—their anomie and depression—really help in the long term. I'm also not sure what *does* help. Is it accepting one's personality, talents, and strengths and weaknesses? Learning to accept oneself is a lifelong journey, one that for Jim and Katie hasn't been easy.

9

. . .

Lingering Impressions

Does ADHD Matter in the Long Term?

Research articles published in peer-reviewed academic journals have a standard format: introduction, methods, results, and conclusions. Before the authors venture their conclusions, there's usually a paragraph or two qualifying or limiting their findings based on their methodology. When I began assembling material for this book, I was very clear that the "findings" of my project would not—and were not meant to—meet the standards of academic medical research. I didn't include a specific non-ADHD community control group for comparison purposes, so I couldn't rigorously contrast my ADHD patients' outcomes with those of "normal" kids.

Thirteen years ago, neither did I use standardized assessment tools (questionnaires or structured interviews) to diagnose ADHD in the children I profiled in *Running on Ritalin*. I may have been biased in my assessments, but if anything, my standards for applying the ADHD label were probably tougher than those used by most other medical professionals. The treatment protocols I employed were based on my training and experience, which could, I admit, be described as idiosyncratic.

I am a family-systems-oriented pediatrician who strongly endorses the belief that inherent temperament and personality are major components of children's behavior. I also believe that children have inherent talents and weaknesses that may encompass extremes of learning or processing disorders as well as average to above-average intelligence. While the use of medication can be a very useful short-term—or even long-term—intervention, it is unlikely to change long-term outcomes, in my estimation. However, before prescribing drugs, I am deeply committed to first offering parents and teachers behavioral management strategies and educational interventions to attempt to address issues in the child's environment.

I work in the real world of clinical practice; my mission is solely to solve problems and alleviate suffering. While there are patterns to my diagnostic and therapeutic practices, each treatment was (and is) tailored to a specific child, family, and school. In contrast, academic research treatments are standardized and include control groups to determine the relative effectiveness, safety, and costs of various approaches.

In my earlier book, *Running on Ritalin*, I specifically selected "subjects" who would highlight aspects of the ADHD/ADD diagnosis and treatment that I thought were important in the mid-1990s. For this book, I chose those who were now in their mid-twenties or older, and because I believe academic stress to be a major factor in the use of Ritalin in children, I wanted those with whom I was following up to have completed most of their mandatory education, which today means college.

I believe academic stress to be a major factor in the use of Ritalin in children.

As it turns out, given the current economic context, many of these young adults were still dependent—in whole or in part—on their parents for funds or housing. At the time I caught up to my former patients, most were on the cusp of truly independent living. None had married and none was raising children. One can only speculate on how their perceptions and needs may alter as their living situations and responsibilities, especially to others, change. Specifically, will they feel the desire or need to return to Ritalin?

I am uneasy using words such as "findings" or "conclusions" in this discussion. They sound too absolute, and I know they will be challenged. I'll leave the science of adult ADHD/ADD to my friend and colleague, Russell Barkley. But whatever the limitations of my informal study, I believe that several of its aspects have utility for parents of today's ADHD/ADD children and the young adults who have used medication in the past or are currently employing or considering psychiatric drugs.

I've already mentioned that the children of *Running on Ritalin* came from middle- and upper-middle-class families. I saw them in a private practice, which meant that the parents either had enough money to pay me out of pocket or had jobs that provided mental health insurance. As I mentioned in Chapter 2, Russell Barkley acknowledged that his pool of ADHD candidates and community controls came from a lower-middle-class/Medicaid population. Readers can decide which patient population best fits their situation and make the necessary adjustments when applying the respective outcomes of our work to their own situations.

Specific treatments utilized for each child and his or her circumstances also reflect experiences different from university research. Readers will have to determine how closely my approaches coincide with theirs. Obviously, I'm attached to my approaches, both theoretically and personally. I think I'm good at what I do. I also know that, in the real world, it would be dif-

The "Heisenberg uncertainty principle" of behavioral research: The observer influences the observed.

ficult to find an MD still committed to nondrug interventions for children with ADHD. Nevertheless, parents of today's children can seek a mix of professional assistance that is congruent with the combination of educational, behavioral, and drug strategies almost universally advocated by experts.

Finally, I must acknowledge the "Heisenberg uncertainty principle" of behavioral research: The observer influences the observed. Unless researchers are "blind" to the type of treatment that was provided, their questions and expectations can bias the subjects' responses. In the case of those I interviewed, I knew them well when they were children and adolescents. Over time, they are likely to have tuned into my biases, either consciously or unconsciously. So, both as their former doctor and contemporary interviewer, I may have influenced their responses.

> I was frequently stunned (and deeply affected) by their candor and willingness to share with me their most personal triumphs and failures.

Still, I believe that my intimate knowledge of their lives led them to give me honest answers to highly personal, core questions. I was frequently stunned (and deeply affected) by their candor and willingness to share with me their most personal triumphs and failures. Again, readers can determine the value of my highly impressionistic responses to the stories of people whom I knew so well.

Notwithstanding these limitations, I offer the following impressions, which linger from these conversations with my now-adult former patients:

- *In childhood, persistence and intensity are bigger problems than the impulsivity, distractibility, and hyperactivity of ADHD.*

We all know the prevailing zeitgeist about childhood ADHD. It is a genetic/biochemical/brain-based disorder that potentially requires treatment (drugs) for life. Based on thirty years of treating children in the middle-class social strata, I sensed that that was true for only a minority of children. My experience with the young adults of *Remembering Ritalin* reinforces this opinion.

I've come to believe that the problems of children to whom the ADHD/ADD label is applied have less to do with impulsivity, distractibility, inattention, and sometimes hyperactivity than to the personality attributes of persistence and intensity. These characteristics make compliance more difficult. I define "compliance" as doing something that you don't want to do but are required to do by an exterior force. Learning compliance is a fundamental process and a developmental hurdle faced by children in every human society.

A child who is persistent by nature—who doesn't give up easily and is determined or stubborn—requires more immediate, consistent, and confident parenting and limit setting. And a child with an intense temperament—who forcefully expresses both positive and negative internal emotional states—also poses greater challenges to compliance and limit setting. Unless parents are prepared to deal steadily and firmly with the child's high levels of negative response, problems of compliance are likely to develop.

Basically, parents bring children to see doctors like me because the children are having problems with compliance (and/or for academic performance problems, which are also compliance issues, since children are required to go to school and learn). Even when children are not directly oppositional, if the schoolwork or homework

A child who is persistent by nature—who doesn't give up easily and is determined or stubborn—requires more immediate, consistent, and confident parenting and limit setting.

In our country, all forms of misbehavior and underperformance are candidates for the ADHD/ADD diagnosis.

isn't completed, they are not in compliance with their environment's social expectations. That is not to say that impulsivity, distractibility, and hyperactivity aren't problems in their own right. But honestly, in my experience, without persistence and intensity, these qualities are rarely problematic.

In our country, all forms of misbehavior and underperformance are candidates for the ADHD/ADD diagnosis. For example, I am nonplussed that noncompliant persistence (labeled "hyperfocusing") has become part of the unofficial catechism of attention *deficit* disorder. A child who is hyperfocusing is tuning into selected tasks or projects rather than doing what the parent or teacher wants him or her to do. In my opinion, the inclusion of hyperfocusing within the ADHD lexicon is an obvious contradiction. It is, however, routinely accepted by parents and doctors. In the final analysis, the solution—Ritalin and related drugs—helps everyone stick with tasks they find boring or difficult, but it will not turn a "no" into a "yes." Still, most children have enough ambivalence about compliance and enough of a desire to please that even those who are persistent and intense will behave more conventionally when they take the drug.

ADHD's high comorbidity rates of oppositional behavior and learning problems attest to official psychiatry's attempt to describe the real world of parenting and educating children. Extreme hyperactivity and impulsivity alone constitute enough of a problem to justify the use of medication. My informal estimate is that about 10 percent of the children receiving medication (both in my practice and throughout the United States) fall into this category.

Again, I have no problem employing medication after reasonable attempts have been made to address the child's problems with the nondrug interventions of behavior modification and special education. But the pediatric and psychiatric professional guidelines that promote Ritalin as a first and only treatment for ADHD have opted for efficiency over engagement. They represent a limited diagnostic perspective and don't address the broader world of real children.

In my opinion, the inclusion of hyperfocusing within the ADHD lexicon is an obvious contradiction.

• *For young, middle-class adults, the importance of ADHD/ADD diminishes after high school.*

There is widespread agreement that the hyperactivity of childhood ADHD gradually wanes and disappears around puberty and during the early teenage years. In fact, until the 1980s, doctors routinely halted Ritalin treatment about that time because the most visible aspects of the disorder were no longer present.

Then, our recognition that the impulsivity, inattention, distractibility, disorganization, and procrastination of ADHD/ADD lasted into the teenage years prompted us to continue prescribing Ritalin to patients beyond the age of thirteen. It wasn't until the mid-1990s that ADHD became fixed in the professional literature and the public's mind as a lifelong disorder requiring treatment.

I have immense respect for Russell Barkley and his research. He, more than anyone, has endeavored to define ADHD/ADD, which I believe is like searching for the Holy Grail (seeking and striving but never finding). It's important work. However, I feel his conclusions about the long-term outcomes of ADHD, which are based on legitimate prospective data from his Milwaukee children's group, have been tainted by data from his UMass Adult Clinic. The

I have immense respect for Russell Barkley and his research.

information coming from the UMass group inevitably retains some inherently negative biases associated with patients who come in for the treatment of a current problem.

Furthermore, as mentioned now many times, Barkley's clinical and control cohorts in the Milwaukee group came from a lower socioeconomic stratum than the middle-class children in my informal cohort. Barkley and I agreed that my group's generally better outcomes conformed to those of his H– group and were likely the result of better support as well as treatment of ADHD's companion disorders of ODD and learning disabilities.

When I talked to the young adults profiled in this book, most of whom were impulsive and hyperactive and had had years of treatment with Ritalin, they told me they still felt "ADHD" in some ways. They could still be impulsive at times and sometimes had trouble following through or focusing their attention. But virtually all of them considered these problems to be manageable and/or controllable without Ritalin. A number even found these characteristics to have useful aspects—expressed, for example, in Cameron's entrepreneurial risk-taking behavior or Bobby's easygoing and joyous attitude toward life.

Nearly all of these young adults who took Ritalin as children experienced side effects they didn't like. But overall, they said that—within the context of their treatment—the decision to use Ritalin was correct and helpful. They felt that during a time when they had little choice about what they had to do, it made their lives easier. They also repeatedly mentioned that it was likely they would have gotten into even more trouble without the drug.

Only three of the ten (which includes Jim, who only uses Ritalin sporadically) felt their life problems gave them reasons to be taking the drug today. This says a great deal about their current attitudes. Evan has taken Ritalin-type drugs for thirteen years, but I'm not certain how much of his decision reflects his perfectionist and inertia-prone personality. Jim uses it occasionally as a specific performance enhancer. Katie just restarted Adderall, but again, I can't say for sure to what degree she was influenced by a true failure to complete tasks based on her problems with distractibility and disorganization as opposed to her very high standards and general dissatisfaction with herself.

The behavior and attitudes of Kevin and Daniel, felon and future policeman, respectively, worry me enough to believe that their impulsivity could still be a problem for them; perhaps they *should* still be taking Ritalin. Daniel, at least, has found an occupation that has external hierarchy and structure, while Kevin's military career ended in a discharge for "false enlistment." It's ironic that the two young adults I thought to be the likeliest candidates for medication were also the two least likely to take it. Similar, I assume, are the tragic individuals in Barkley's H+ group and the many people with extreme ADHD who end up incarcerated.

I cannot predict who, if any, of these young adults, now not using Ritalin, will return to Ritalin in the future—when as older adults, job and family responsibilities increase. However, I also cannot predict how their personalities may mature and rise to the increased demands of work, marriage, and parenthood.

Not withstanding Kevin's current status, my follow-up with the individuals I knew as children thirteen years ago reassures me that their outcomes are better than what academics preach and the general public believes. I can hardly believe that these improved outcomes are solely the result of my treatment (though candidly, I have to say I'm quite pleased to have been associated with these young adults). Rather, they did better because their families could offer them more and better treatments (both drug and nondrug) and support than could the families of children associated with the long-term ADHD academic research.

• *Nature, nurture, and the quality of the experience.*

I first met Kevin when he was seven, Sam and Lauren at eleven, Jim at sixteen, and Katie at seventeen. With all of them, I was struck with the consistency of their personalities from childhood to age twenty-six or older. For Kevin, his anger was the constant, and for Sam, it was his interpersonal struggles. As a child, Lauren blamed others and did so as an adult as well. Jim and Katie were still so tough on themselves. I felt bad for all of them and wondered whether I could have done more for them.

The nature-versus-nurture controversy is ongoing. Barkley and others take the position that ADHD is essentially a "nature" issue, with a heritability factor of 0.8 (roughly equivalent to a parent's genetic contribution to the ultimate adult height of his or her child). I agree with Barkley that elements of personality and temperament, including impulsivity and distractibility, are likely to be inherited. But as I've said, for the kids whom I followed, I'm not sure that the ADHD/ADD characteristics they may have inherited from their parents were as critical as other inherited qualities such as persistence and intensity.

Bobby was intense (and very hyperactive), but somehow, things started improving for him in high school; at twenty-six, he has a positive attitude that is quite infectious. You could say that his personality hadn't changed either. Neither Jennifer nor Cameron liked being told what to do, but now they are their own bosses, and their determination is taking them to better places.

I don't think you can alter a child's personality. A dozen years ago, psychologist Judith Harris published *The Nurture Assumption:*

Why Children Turn Out the Way They Do. One more brick in the biological wall, her research indicated that ultimately, children are a product of genes and biology. Much of her work and conclusions were based on long-term studies of identical twins reared apart, in particular the Minnesota Twin Studies, which are ongoing (the subjects are now in their forties).

> I don't think you can alter a child's personality.

Reviewers and critics vilified Harris, charging that in her book, she was saying that "parenting doesn't matter." Rather, Harris was only explaining in lay terms what those researching the influence of genetics and environment on the development of psychological traits had concluded: Except in cases of abuse and neglect, by age twenty-five, identical twins adopted separately and reared apart were remarkably similar not only physically but also emotionally and even in their interests, likes, and dislikes.

Harris provided the following example to explain what the research truly said about children and the environment: If you marry with the idea that you can fundamentally change your spouse's personality, most people would consider you both wrong and naïve. However, the way you and your spouse treat one another can make a big difference in the quality of your relationship. Harris said, and I agree, that parents should view their relationships with their children the same way.

Short of the extremes of abuse and neglect, the way parents raise their children may not alter their personalities and achievements. By their mid-twenties, they will turn out to be very similar to their parents. However, how parents act with their children, what they provide, and how they respond to them may greatly influence the quality and experiences the children have on their way to their ultimate outcomes.

Fortunately, as I have said, the vast majority of the parents I meet have jobs and relatively stable relationships, and the outcomes for their children will be similarly positive. My role is to help these parents develop ways to ameliorate or soften the bumps on child-hood's road.

- *Well, then, Dr. Diller, if parenting doesn't make a long-term difference, how do you explain the better outcomes for your patients?*

There are two answers. First, the better outcomes are once again explained by the socioeconomic differences—and whatever that implies about parents' intelligence, temperament, and interventions—between the parents of the children in my group and those of the academic studies.

Furthermore, any studies of twins in which the twins were ad-opted automatically exclude the worst emotional and economic en-vironments common to children raised in poverty or with racial prejudice. Adoptive parents are routinely screened for severe emo-tional or marital problems and must also be deemed economically capable of caring for their adoptive children. Thus, I strongly be-lieve that extreme deprivation will have a negative impact on chil-dren's long-term outcome.

Given my acceptance of the idea that personality is relatively fixed, I continue to wonder if I could have done anything different for my former patients who were still struggling. James Satterfield thought that perhaps intervening in the preschool years might have made a difference in the long-term negative outcomes he found for children with ADHD and behavior problems. Responding to the power of genes, some doctors propose early and lifelong medication for children with these problems. I could make the case that im-proving their desperate environments would work equally well. But from a public health/societal point of view, we don't lack the means to make a difference—we lack the will.

- *Generation Rx is finding its professional and personal niches.*

Over and over, I found that the young adults of *Remembering Ritalin* who were happiest were those who found jobs and relationships that worked for them. During our mid-twenties, compliance is still an issue. There are bosses to deal with and classes not entirely of one's choosing to take. But on a daily basis, these young adults had much more choice about what they were doing.

Here I think of Sam in higher mathematics, Jennifer in employment counseling, Evan as a car mechanic, Daniel as a police officer, Cameron as an entrepreneur, Bobby as an artist and community organizer. Even Katie—who was, I believe, unhappy for other reasons—was still quite successful as an artist and teacher. All of them struggled in school, especially with their impulsivity and distractibility. All were entirely capable, even as children, of focusing on things they were interested in or liked. Now, as adults, they are able to choose where to direct their attention and energy. Using my children's sorting toy model of ADHD, they have found the correctly shaped holes for their uniquely shaped temperaments and talents. They no longer require Ritalin as a lubricant to help them fit.

Now, as adults, they are able to choose where to direct their attention and energy.

Finding personal and community niches also seemed important. Bobby's discovery of San Francisco's artistic/gay community virtually changed his view of himself overnight. Jennifer seemed to thrive in the counseling community and with the connections she had made with her boyfriend and their extended social network.

In contrast, Sam—with all his mathematical talents—still sounded wistful about relationships and connections. He struggled with his shyness and lack of a meaningful relationship or social network. Evan was quite happy with his work, but a bit embarrassed that, despite his respectable income, he still lived at home with his parents. I am confident that eventually, well-intentioned women will find Sam and Evan, recognize their dependability and loyalty, and choose them as mates. For the young adults of *Remembering Ritalin*, the connections they make with friends and lovers will prove even more important to their happiness than the jobs they have found.

• *Remembering me in* Remembering Ritalin.

The year I worked on this book changed me. After thirty-two years in practice, I consider myself about two-thirds of the way through a career in behavioral-developmental pediatrics. This project afforded me a unique opportunity to check up on the progress of these young adults, the first Generation Rx-ers to come of age. I look forward to staying in touch with them as they move into stable jobs and family relationships of their own.

I've learned a couple of things about the way I practice. Hearing Cameron tell me how much he hated having his mother say bad things about him in the office reinforced my commitment to allay this concern. I now insist that parents talk directly to their children rather than to me when they want to "report in" on family progress or problems.

That having been said, I don't know how much it would have helped Cameron if his parents had observed that rule. Children feel responsible for their family's problems and it's unlikely anything can entirely eliminate those feelings. But I've never felt comfortable when parents—intentionally or unintentionally—act as though their children weren't present or don't have feelings about the problems or "crimes" in which they're involved. When parents talk directly to their child, they are acknowledging the child's presence and providing a more natural opportunity for the child to respond or even defend him- or herself.

On a positive note, I was gratified by the number of young adults who told me they had liked coming to my office. They had good memories of playing with their parents or with me. Though I no longer do play therapy, my meetings with parents and children routinely include some games or time for playing with toys. I don't do this simply to give children a good time. All the interactions in my office, including play, are subject to my analysis and potential intervention. I am recommitted to using play with families as part of my evaluation and treatment.

All but one of the young adults of *Remembering Ritalin* told me they thought the Ritalin I had prescribed for them was helpful at the time. Some of them went to great lengths to let me know they appreciated the way I described the medication's action: as an aid to making better decisions, which they nonetheless had to make on their own. Schoolwork could be more easily completed. They'd have more time to think through a decision before reacting. But the decision to do the schoolwork or take the proper action remained theirs.

All of them told me that my efforts to address their family's issues were even more important to them. While I didn't necessarily solve their problems, they all said that their time with me helped their family at least move in a better direction. I wish more families had access to counselors who work specifically on parenting issues and, if necessary, invest in a long-term exploration with parents of their own moods and marriages. Too many nondrug treatments are still oriented to play therapy directed to the child. Too little is offered to the parents in terms of direct advice and support in raising these often very difficult children.

Finally, with this project, I recognized the limits of my interventions. While I have confidence that most of the children I meet will ultimately turn out like their parents—in other words, productive citizens—I still feel bad that I can't influence their life's course more profoundly in terms of happiness and satisfaction. The notion of a physician as more of a spectator than a participant rings all the more true for me since undertaking this project.

In the end, however, my resolve to improve children's lives remains unaltered, and the recognition of my limitations humbles me.

10

· · ·

Potpourri

Answering Some Common Questions
About ADHD/ADD and Ritalin

I offer this extended "bonus" chapter to explore aspects of ADHD/
ADD and Ritalin that weren't specifically covered by the interviews
with and commentary on the young adults of *Remembering Ritalin*.
Parents of ADHD/ADD children or candidates for the diagnosis
(perhaps 10 to 15 percent of school-age children in the United
States) will find this section of particular interest. Many of the topics covered have to do with evaluation and treatment.

Adults who have taken medication as children, currently use
psychiatric drugs, or are considering meds for ADHD will also
find some of the topics to be of interest. Finally, this chapter explores how the economic and professional powers embedded in
our nation's educational and health care systems do not always
serve the best interests of children with learning and behavioral
differences.

Behavioral health care disorder:
Is the mental health system biased toward Ritalin?

The Hastings Center, founded in 1969, is the oldest and one of the most prestigious bioethics think tanks in the world; I also consider it my medical ethics "home base." Their journal, the *Hastings Center Report*, published my first major article on ADHD and Ritalin ("The Run on Ritalin") in 1996 after I had spent nearly three years trying to place it in a professional medical journal. That led to a request by the *New York Times* for an article about Ritalin and, ultimately, to my first book contract for *Running on Ritalin*, which was published in 1998.

So, at the request of Erik Parens of the Hastings Center, I was thrilled to participate in a series of meetings on aspects of specific diagnoses, such as ADHD or bipolar disorder and their treatments. The sessions were approved and funded by the National Institutes of Mental Health (NIMH) and sponsored by the center.

Following the 2008–2009 symposia, I awaited with great anticipation the first publications coming from these meetings. I was not disappointed. A special supplement to the *Hastings Center Report*, scheduled to be published in 2011, attempted the near impossible: to summarize and achieve a reasonable consensus among the thirty or so participants of the five separate conferences. The supplement, which ran twenty pages, made three essential points:

- "Reasonable people will disagree" over diagnostic issues. The authors recognized that within the United States and the rest of the world, there will be continued disagreement on diagnosis, particularly on behaviors in a "zone of ambiguity." Such problematic behavior could reasonably be interpreted as simply a variation or extreme of normal, or a mild disorder. Because of the nature of psychiatric diagnosis (no biological or psychometric markers), some disagreement is inevitable and to be expected.

• People will also disagree over values associated with the use of medications versus nondrug interventions for children's psychiatric disorders. The use of pills highlights values of "efficiency" (money and time) while the nondrug interventions emphasize "engagement" with the child (counseling, special education, and so forth). Efficiency and engagement succinctly and precisely summarize the difference in values between the two approaches.

• Finally, the article concludes that the behavioral health delivery system in our country—which, for children, includes doctors (psychiatrists and pediatricians), psychologists, hospitals, and therapists, and the reimbursements they receive— tilts interventions toward the use of medication rather than nondrug options. I would add that our current educational system also provides the academic pressures that provoke the majority of referrals of children to the medical and mental health system for medication.

I believe, and the *Hastings Center Report* agrees, that money and the power interests inherent in our medical delivery system have a bias for efficiency over engagement in the delivery of services to children.

I've used my own satiric Swiftian "Modest Proposal" to highlight the differences in values associated with different means (methods) even when the ends (results) may be equivalent: With classroom size averaging thirty children per class, and four million children taking Ritalin, I propose that we increase the number

Money and the power interests inherent in our medical delivery system have a bias for efficiency over engagement in the delivery of services to children.

taking Ritalin to seven million so that we can then increase classroom size to forty children per class. With this change, we could save a lot of money on teachers' salaries and school buildings.

People snicker when they hear this, and no politician or leader could ever voice such an idea without being booted out of office. Yet, every day in America, this is exactly what we do when we offer children Ritalin as the first and only treatment and don't attempt to address issues of behavior and school performance with equally effective but costlier nondrug interventions.

I have no illusions that calls for more money to keep classroom size small, provide special education and behavioral interventions in school, or support more parenting therapies are likely to be heeded. Still, I must raise my voice, for not to do so makes me, as a doctor who prescribes Ritalin, complicit in practices and values I believe are bad for children. While it was gratifying to read the Hastings Center supplement report, and I felt my concerns about Ritalin had been validated, I recognize that even this report is unlikely to lead to major changes in the way we deliver care to our children.

What are the most common prescribing errors when using Ritalin with children?

Over the years, I've regularly inherited patients who had been started on Ritalin and other stimulant medications and had been on a very low dose for years. Their doctors prescribed a fixed dose of the medication, say, 10 milligrams. The children improved somewhat, and the medication was considered a success.

There is no weight-based (milligram of dose per kilogram of weight) dosing schedule for Ritalin. Rather, dosage is based solely on clinical response; a five-year-old boy could take the same dose as a forty-year-old man. When beginning a stimulant medication, a child should undergo a titration trial, and every three to five days, the dose should be increased by the smallest available pill size until the level that works best for the child is determined.

For example, Concerta's lowest available dosage is 18 milligrams. For the first three to five days, the child takes one pill; the next three to five days, two pills (36 milligrams); and for the last period, three pills (54 milligrams) simultaneously. In an ideal situation, teachers use a daily feedback form (shown below) on which they grade the child on behaviors such as impulsivity, inattention, and work completion. The teacher does this evaluation blindly— without knowledge of the specific dosage the child is taking. The goal is to achieve the best performance without side effects.

There is no weight-based (milligram of dose per kilogram of weight) dosing schedule for Ritalin.

Name of Child _____

Name of Teacher _____

Date/Day	Dosage		a.m.		p.m.	
			Least *Most*		*Least* *Most*	
		Impulsivity	0 1 2 3		0 1 2 3	
		Distractibility	0 1 2 3		0 1 2 3	
		Incomplete Tasks	0 1 2 3		0 1 2 3	

Comments:

_____

_____

_____

In reality, 18 milligrams is rarely an optimal dosage. So many times, I've met children who have been on the medication for years at this suboptimal level. Both the American Academy of Pediatrics (AAP) and the American Academy of Child and Adolescent Psychiatry (AACAP) recommend this simple titration trial.

Another common dosing mistake made by nonspecialist MDs is using multiple daily doses of short-acting Ritalin or generic methylphenidate. Multiple doses lead to noncompliance, greater stigma, and uneven coverage (multiple "ups and downs" during the day). There are many long-acting versions of methylphenidate and amphetamine now on the market; some last up to twelve hours. Concerta, Adderall XR, Metadate CD, Focalin XR, and Vyvanse are among the long-acting types. If swallowing a capsule is a problem, Adderall XR and Metadate CD can be opened up and added to small amounts of food. And Adderall XR has a very similar generic alternative, so in my opinion, cost isn't a justifiable reason for multiple dosing.

Why use medium-length stimulants for school-day-only coverage?

There are now more than a dozen preparations of stimulant medications commercially available in the United States. Ritalin, Adderall, and Concerta are the best known; Concerta and the XR version of Adderall are promoted as lasting ten to twelve hours. This duration is considered an advantage, as a single dose will last through the school day and into the afternoon for homework completion, which, for very impulsive or distractible children, is ideal. Many of these more expensive, highly profitable drugs have been vigorously promoted by their manufacturers, and this promotion affects the choices of both consumers *and* doctors.

On the downside, these longer-lasting preparations tend to

have a more pronounced negative effect on children's appetite for their evening meal as well as their ability to fall asleep at night. But since many parents are primarily interested in helping their child cope with behavior and performance issues during the school day, these side effects are not necessarily deal breakers.

Methylin ER, a methylphenidate-based preparation available as a generic, is a pill that fills the bill as a school-day-only medicine. It generally lasts six to eight hours and can be taken just before the start of the school day; it then wears off around midafternoon. Dexedrine Spansule, an amphetamine-based medication, also lasts for approximately the length of a school day. Because these pills are generics, they do not get the marketing exposure given to the newer, more expensive, and longer-lasting preparations. Consequently, many parents (and even doctors) are unaware of them.

Are free samples a social good or profit-driven boondoggle?

Large pharmaceutical companies—Eli Lilly, Johnson and Johnson, Shire—have, over the last twenty years, been among the most profitable corporations in the world. While they proclaim a commitment to research and development, their real expertise is in the marketing and distribution of their products.

Shire Pharmaceuticals, with products such as Adderall, Adderall XR, Vyvanse, and Daytrana (a stimulant delivered through the skin via a patch), dominates ADHD stimulant treatments. All these drugs have had extensive advertising directed both to physicians and the general public. Though they are often heralded as major breakthroughs, they actually have limited advantages to preexisting and less expensive stimulant preparations.

Drug companies regularly offer "free samples" to physicians' offices, ostensibly to provide treatment to those who otherwise

These drugs rarely go to indigent families. might have trouble paying the full costs of these drugs. In fact, these drugs rarely go to indigent families. Rather, families covered by private insurance are started on these medications and, once the samples are depleted, are continued on the more expensive products.

Because stimulant prescriptions are Schedule II (abusable and addictive), the drugs themselves cannot be distributed to physicians' offices. But drug companies have found a way around this legal impediment by giving doctors vouchers, which they can pass along to patients. These vouchers are used to pay for the medications when the prescription is picked up at a pharmacy. I advise you to beware of this marketing ploy, because it primarily produces higher profits to drug companies and higher medical costs to the country.

Over three decades, which new medications have made a real difference?

Probably several hundred new drugs have been developed and marketed over the thirty years of my private clinical practice, but only two have made a real difference in results: Concerta and Prozac.

Concerta was the first true daylong preparation that could be taken once in the morning and would last until dinnertime. Before Concerta, children would have to go to a nurse or principal's office around lunchtime for their second dose of Ritalin, which lasted only three to four hours. Many also took a third midafternoon dose when they came home from school.

Concerta, introduced in 1999, eliminated much of the hassle factor of multiple dosings. It also decreased the stigma children might feel about taking medications, as they no longer had to break away from their lunch recess to go to the office for their "crazy pills," as one of my patients put it. Concerta also ended the uneven ups and downs that made it more difficult for children to regulate their behaviors. Subsequent long-acting preparations such as Adderall XR, Metadate CD, Focalin XR, and the highly touted Vyvanse, which supposedly lasts twelve hours, have made little difference in what I actually prescribe.

Prozac was a breakthrough, less for the children I see and more for their parents. Prozac was marketed in 1988 as an antidepressant but, in fact, works more broadly on personality, helping people reduce their sensitivity to irritating stimuli without sedating them. (Valium and vodka will also make one less sensitive, but unfortunately come with sedation, potential tolerance issues, and ultimately addiction.)

Prozac and all the other me-too drugs that followed (Zoloft, Paxil, etc.) were actually no more effective than the older antidepressants such as Elavil or imipramine, but they had fewer side effects and lacked many of the lethal overdose potentials of the older drugs. Indeed, Prozac was responsible for one of the most dramatic public mental health changes: a decrease in the number of Elavil-overdose suicides.

Today, Prozac seems to be used for almost every psychiatric problem.

Today, Prozac seems to be used for almost every psychiatric problem, from depression to anxiety, bulimia, and obsessive-compulsive disorder. Its effectiveness in treating depression in children remains controversial, as does its potential for increasing suicidal thinking. When it comes to childhood anxiety, family-based cognitive behavioral approaches work equally as well as the drug.

Prozac's biggest contribution to my practice was to help the parents of the children I see. Many mothers and fathers achieved an evenness of response with Prozac that is very helpful in the parenting of their children. Notwithstanding sexual side effects (decreased libido and trouble achieving orgasm) that are common to the drug, over the years, many adults have benefited from taking Prozac.

Urban Legend I:
Ritalin's Paradoxical Effect on Hyperactive Children

It began in 1937, when Charles Bradley, a neurologist, described for the first time the effects of amphetamine on children's hyperactive behavior. Bradley was trying to alleviate the severe headaches associated with a procedure that is now considered barbaric: a form of brain scan called pneumoencephalography, in which air is injected through the spinal column into the brain, which is then x-rayed.

While amphetamines didn't eliminate children's headaches, Bradley astutely recognized that Benzedrine, the amphetamine preparation of the time, "appeared" to calm hyperactive children. Thus began the belief that stimulant drugs—Benzedrine and, later, Dexedrine or Ritalin, which otherwise sped people up—"paradoxically" and uniquely calmed children with ADHD. From that observation, people concluded that the ADHD brain is somehow different from the normal brain. Though decades of research have been undertaken in the search for a consistent anatomical or biochemical difference, as yet, nothing has been found.

In fact, a child with ADHD does not respond to stimulant drugs in a unique or different way as compared to a child without these problematic behaviors. Even in the 1930s, people were using the concentrating effects of amphetamine (in low doses) with and without a doctor's prescription. (This phenomenon is being repeated on a massive scale in today's colleges and probably in the business world, too.)

It took the efforts of a National Institutes of Mental Health scientist Judith Rappaport, in the early 1980s, to definitively prove that amphetamine works the same on children with and without ADHD. She gave 10 milligrams of Dexedrine to children with ADHD and 10 milligrams to those without. (Ethical considerations regarding children as research subjects were different then; the researchers used their own children as controls and gave them the drug!) Both groups improved their ability to do repetitive, boring tasks; children with ADHD approached normal performance standards, and the children without the condition operated at supranormal levels. Both groups also became less physically active, but the differences were more noticeable in the hyperactive group.

Thus, a decrease in activity level is not really a result of the "calming" effects of stimulant drugs. Calming implies sedation. Parents and their children often believe the drugs are sedating (a further comment on that in a moment). Rather, at low dosages, the medication makes both children and adults more deliberate and more focused. It is believed the hyperactivity decreases because children are able to maintain interest in or perseverance with a task longer and are less distracted and impulsive when taking the medication.

At low dosages, the medication makes both children and adults more deliberate and more focused.

Even Bradley qualified his original observations by using the word "appears," as in "appears to calm." Methodical and deliberate can look like calmness. But if the dose is increased, at some point hyperactive children will become even more hyperactive, just like the "speed freaks" who abuse the drugs.

One more word on the "sedating" effects of Ritalin: Even in low doses, amphetamine-type drugs can flatten affect in some children, who will seem less emotional and may speak in a robotic style. The effect can be quite noticeable. The children seem weird or drugged.

While this is not the result of sedation, these effects are hardly desirable. When this "flatness" occurs, the dose is usually reduced, or the drug is discontinued and another stimulant is tried.

Finally, the misconception that Ritalin worked differently in children with ADHD led to the long-held belief, which is still operative in some circles, that the drug could be employed as a diagnostic tool; for example, if she improves with Ritalin, then she must have ADHD. That kind of thinking would lead to everyone "having" ADHD, since nearly all will improve their capacity to do boring and repetitive tasks when they take the drug. My sense is that in the last decade, these beliefs are finally ebbing (after seventy years!) but continue to linger among poorly informed patients and doctors.

Urban Legend II: Sugar Causes Children to Become Hyper

The belief that refined sugars cause children to become hyperactive, impulsive, and distractible—the very symptoms that make up the core of ADHD behaviors—is alive and well in the United States.

This belief, held by many parents and teachers, has led to the elimination of food and beverage products that contain refined sugar from children's diets. While there may be very good reasons to reduce or eliminate sugar from what children eat—say, to reduce the obesity epidemic or prevent dental caries—changing children's behavior is not one of them.

The sugar-behavior connection, which has been with us for decades, has been the subject of several elegant studies that have clearly shown that adults perceive their children as more hyperactive after consuming sugar because they believe the connection to be true. Call it disorder by attribution.

My favorite is a study designed by a group headed by Richard

Milich, a noted ADHD researcher; it was published in 1994. In it, thirty-five mother-son pairs were recruited; in each case, the boys were "known" to be sugar-sensitive. The groups were split as follows. The first group was given a Kool-Aid drink, which the mothers were told was sweetened with refined sugar. The second group was also given Kool-Aid, but was told the drink had been sweetened with aspartame (Nutrasweet). In actuality, aspartame was used to sweeten the drink for both groups.

Then, the mothers and sons were asked to work together on a number of puzzles; with the adults' permission, these sessions were videotaped. Experts who didn't know which pairs had been told the truth then reviewed the tapes. Not surprisingly, mothers of the group told that their sons had ingested sugar reported that their children were more unruly, rambunctious, and hyperactive than the mothers who believed their boys had ingested the artificial sweetener.

The big surprise came from the experts' analyses. They rated the boys whose mothers were under the mistaken belief that sugar was involved as *less* hyperactive than the boys whose mothers had been told the truth. Further analysis showed that the mothers of the first group more rigidly controlled their children, who were consequently less active. Apparently, these mothers believed their sons would act worse under the influence of the sugar. The mothers who knew their children took aspartame were more relaxed, and as a result, these boys were a bit more active and lively.

While other laborious studies have been made on the behavior-sugar connection, *none* has demonstrated a difference, ADHD or not. There is a bit of evidence that—in enor-

I continue to maintain that I'd rather have parents do battle with their children over whether or not they put away their toys than whether or not they eat a cupcake.

mous quantities—chemical food colorings can make children more irritable and restless. While it is indeed possible that diet may have a small effect on some children, sugar isn't the culprit.

I continue to maintain that I'd rather have parents do battle with their children over whether or not they put away their toys than whether or not they eat a cupcake. I suggest parents save their energies for the conflicts that will make a difference in their children's behavior. But I have no illusions that the sugar-affects-behavior myth will ever disappear entirely.

Urban Legend III:
Alternative Treatments for ADHD Are Effective

Among the questions I've been asked is that, if I am so reluctant to use Ritalin in children, why am I not a bigger advocate of the alternative and complementary medical interventions for ADHD? First of all, I am not reluctant to use Ritalin, but I do believe it should not be the first and only intervention for ADHD children. I do not support interventions such as dietary restrictions, health and herbal products, or biofeedback, to name just a few of the current alternatives, because they have not been demonstrated to be effective.

The wish for non-Ritalin alternatives is so great that a huge complementary and alternative industry exists to cater to these hopes.

Yes, there have been any number of small, uncontrolled studies that show benefits to dietary protocols and biofeedback. But none of these studies has been published in major medical journals such as the *Journal of the American Medical Association* (*JAMA*), the *New England Journal of Medicine* (*NEJM*), *Pediatrics*, *Neurology*, or the *Journal of the American Academy of*

Child and Adolescent Psychiatry (JAACAP). All these journals have high standards for publication that require studies to incorporate large numbers of children enrolled in methodical and controlled experiments.

Case reports and nonblinded studies without a well-matched control group are notorious for delivering the results for which the researchers were expecting or hoping. The public greatly desires the development of effective non-Ritalin interventions for ADHD. Worries about Ritalin persist despite seventy years of its safe and effective use in children. The wish for non-Ritalin alternatives is so great that a huge complementary and alternative industry exists to cater to these hopes.

Conceptually, since ADHD is brain-mediated, biofeedback should work. Research results have been tantalizing at times, but not definitive. Should there be a definitive study published in a major medical journal, we would all learn about it simultaneously because it would appear in major newspaper headlines, on TV, and in Internet news outlets. That's how desperate the public is for an alternative. But until such a study is published—biofeedback has been used in ADHD for over twenty years, so there's been time—I suggest the caveat emptor (buyer beware) approach to these interventions.

Similarly, over the course of my career, I've seen many herbal and health food products or elimination diets come and go from public consciousness: the Feingold diet (among other things, oranges and tomatoes are eliminated—no pizza!); antioxidants such as pycnogenol; and the current popularity of omega-3 fatty acids and gluten-free diets. Again, there are some intriguing results with omega-3 capsules and behavior (up to six capsules are required daily), but nothing definitive has been published.

I suppose swallowing up to six pills a day, if not bothersome, won't take as much time or money as biofeedback. But I'm still waiting for results. In the meantime, I will support the nondrug interventions that have proven effective for ADHD—behavioral modification and special education approaches—and then use Ritalin if there are still major problems.

How important is it for fathers to participate in ADHD diagnosis and treatment plans?

In my practice, I insist on involving fathers in the evaluation and treatment of their children. This was much more difficult in the 1970s when I first began working in behavioral-developmental pediatrics. But even back then, when I requested a father's presence at the first history-taking session, he was usually there.

If the father can't make the first visit, I generally insist that he take part in the one family session I routinely conduct to evaluate family dynamics. If the mother reports that her spouse is unavailable or not interested, I'll ask for her permission to speak to her husband directly. I'd estimate that, of the dozens of times I've made this request, fewer than ten fathers (out of three thousand!) declined to come in to talk to me. In those cases, I considered that the mothers' biggest problems might not be with their children but with their marriages.

> I'd estimate that, of the dozens of times I've made this request, fewer than ten fathers (out of three thousand!) declined to come in to talk to me.

Having fathers participate, especially when they initially disagree with their wives about the severity or nature of their children's problems, enriches my view of the child's world. Furthermore, getting the parents to agree on the diagnosis and participate together in treatment often decreases the need for a medication intervention; if medication is required, it also makes it more effective when both parents are joined in planning and implementation.

What are the pros and cons of using questionnaires to diagnose ADHD?

Questionnaires directed to parents and teachers have become the unintentional sine qua non for diagnosing ADHD in children. Among the most popular are the Achenbach and Connors (named after their creators) and the Vanderbilt (after the university). Official protocols promoted by the AAP and AACAP urge the use of these questionnaires. Why don't I use them in my practice?

The questionnaires are similar in that they include questions such as "How much does your child fidget?" The respondent is asked to choose the most appropriate answer: "never," "rarely," "sometimes," "frequently," or "all the time." The number of "frequently" or "all the time" answers are then tabulated; if the score is high enough, the child's behaviors are deemed potentially problematic, or "within the clinical range."

Those who originated the questionnaires have said that their forms should not be used as the sole basis for an ADHD diagnosis. But because of their convenience (saving time and, therefore, money), in most primary-care practices, the questionnaires are the de facto diagnostic decision makers. In fact, if a doctor obtains completed questionnaires from both parents and the teacher, his or her practice has met the state-of-the-art criteria for an acceptable evaluation for ADHD.

Apart from the logistical appeal of using the questionnaires, I appreciate that they offer some standardization to this "eye-of-the-beholder" diagnosis of a disorder that has no other biological or psychometric markers. But I have three main beefs about their use. First, they reflect the current contextless position on symptoms maintained by the

The questionnaires reveal nothing about the subjective attitudes and biases of those who answer the questions.

Diagnostic and Statistical Manual of Mental Disorders (DSM-IV). There could be many reasons why a child fidgets excessively, including anxiety, trauma, hunger, and so forth. Yet neither the *DSM* nor the questionnaires make these distinctions.

Second, the questionnaires reveal nothing about the subjective attitudes and biases of those who answer the questions. Rather than relying on a teacher's responses to a form, I prefer to spend between ten and fifteen minutes on the telephone with him or her, discussing the student's behavior at school. In the process of learning about the child, I can also make some judgments about the teacher's attitudes and practices in general and, specifically, about ADHD.

The cynical response to the question "Which children do best on the questionnaires?" is "Dead children," because they don't do anything wrong.

Finally, the questionnaires only focus on the *degree* of weaknesses demonstrated by the child. When I speak to the teacher, this is my initial question: "Tell me about this child's strengths and weaknesses, academically and behaviorally." I specifically inquire about strengths to get a full profile. The cynical response to the question "Which children do best on the questionnaires?" is "Dead children," because they don't do anything wrong.

By only asking about negative behaviors, the questionnaires unintentionally but universally require the respondents to focus on the negative at the expense of the positive. While clearly attention needs to be paid to problem behaviors, I prefer to be solution-focused. Therefore, I eschew questionnaires and instead speak to parents and teachers and, in the process, am able to form an opinion about the adults' attitudes. All of this allows me to develop a better idea of what's going on and tailor more precise interventions for the child and his or her environment.

Who should attend Individualized Educational Plan (IEP) meetings?

The Individuals with Disabilities Education Act (IDEA) mandates an optimal education tailored to the specific needs of each student. A fairly extensive evaluation—which includes assessments by (at the minimum) the school psychologist, the speech and language pathologist, and the resource teacher—is employed to determine the child's strengths and weaknesses and whether he or she meets the criteria for special education services (especially small-group instruction with a specialist).

The failure of the federal government to fully fund special education mandates has placed school districts in the awkward position of having to raid funds intended for the general classroom to support special education children (whose costs on average are four times that of regular education kids). This cost disequilibrium creates potential tension between the parents, who may want special services, and the school district, which is looking to serve only those kids with the greatest needs in order to save money.

The meetings often take on a quasi-legal air.

This tension between the potential needs of the children and the realities of funding is one reason I tell parents never to attend an IEP meeting without their spouse, a relative, a friend, a neighbor, or a professional advocate like me. Even in the absence of a funding issue, there are usually four or five experts whose first job is to give the parents the test results on their child's performance. For the parent, this can be a tedious, overwhelming experience.

The meetings often take on a quasi-legal air, which can make the process even more uncomfortable for the parent who attends one alone. Granted, any decisions reached and signed off on (literally) can be reviewed at any time at a parent's request. Still, the process

Two sets of eyes and ears, and two brains, are much better than one in these situations.

can be overpowering and intimidating, which is why two sets of eyes and ears, and two brains, are much better than one in these situations.

I've attended several hundred IEP meetings over my three decades in practice and believe the process has evolved into a set of procedures inimical to good communication and consensus. Because the school has a legal obligation to share their findings, parents are bombarded with numbers and data they rarely fully understand. Too often, forty-five minutes of a fifty-minute meeting are devoted to experts sharing their findings, leaving only five minutes to develop a plan to best educate the child.

Despite the potentially adversarial roles involved, I do not often find myself in combat with school officials. For one, I think the parents' decision to have me attend these meetings puts schools on their best behavior. And in general, most schools welcome my participation. They are pleased that the parents have made efforts on their own to address their child's performance or behavior problems. Most of the time, school officials complain to me that the parents of children who need the most help are the ones least likely to obtain outside assistance.

Most of the time at these meetings, I act as a facilitator between the family and the school, maintaining a sense of advocacy for the child and family I've evaluated. I've found that schools rarely miss or misunderstand the true situation. Similarly, I think parents are more relaxed and comfortable when they know they have someone in the room looking out for their child's best interests because it allows them to be better listeners. The vast majority of the time, the process goes smoothly.

I don't attend every IEP meeting, however. Many times my presence really isn't required. Parents have to pay for both the time

I spend at the meeting and a portion of my travel time, so they decide if they want me to attend. Over the last five years, I've often participated via speakerphone, which I find is generally quite adequate. For many reasons, it's preferable to attend in person, but phone conferences are less costly and easier to schedule because I don't have to travel or leave my office between patients. I look forward to the next decade, when videoconferencing will come even to public schools.

Who should evaluate my child for ADHD/ADD?

Given that a virtual ADHD/ADD industry has developed around this diagnosis and its treatment, it shouldn't be too difficult to find someone to evaluate your child for ADHD/ADD in most suburban and urban areas. However, in my experience, ADHD/ADD experts tend to recommend a trial of stimulant medication either right away or very early in the process for the variety of issues that could fall under an ADHD diagnosis but could also be addressed with non-drug interventions.

Your pediatrician or family doctor should be your first source of information and opinion about your child, especially if she has known your family for several years. How-

---

Adults Only: Five Questions to Ask Yourself When Considering the Use of Ritalin

1. Are your goals (academic, professional, and personal) commensurate with your true talents and interests?

2. Are you truly underperforming, or have you set up unrealistic, impossible-to-meet standards?

3. To what degree are the interests of others (parents, spouse, boss) driving your sense of underperformance?

4. Could anxiety and depression be contributing to "poor concentration," with the understanding that poor concentration can make one anxious and depressed?

5. What other measures have you taken (or are you willing to consider taking) before relying on a medication that you may have to use for the rest of your life?

ever, the high overhead costs of a primary-care practice preclude the doctor from spending sufficient time to do an adequate evaluation. Though simple review of ADHD questionnaires (as mentioned earlier) is not enough, this approach has passed official muster as an adequate evaluation.

It's better to ask the doctor to refer you to a specialist, who has time to do a more thorough investigation of your child's educational and behavioral performance. There are many specialists who might fit that bill in your community: child psychiatrists, behavioral-developmental pediatricians, psychologists (educational and neuro-psychologists have further specializations), and other mental health specialists (social workers and marriage, family, and child counselors).

The first question you could ask either your pediatrician or the specialist she refers you to is, "Do you support non-drug interventions for ADHD?"

From my point of view, the first question you could ask either your pediatrician or the specialist she refers you to is, "Do you support nondrug interventions for ADHD, and if so, to what degree?" Pay attention to the answer, because it will give you a clue as to the type of evaluation and practice offered by the specialist. Furthermore, it will let your doctor or the specialist know that you desire to fully explore nondrug interventions before embarking on a medication trial. Despite official recommendations that Ritalin can be employed as a first-line intervention for ADHD/ADD, most specialists are sensitive to the continuing controversies about the drug and overmedication. Ask around until you get an answer with which you are comfortable.

Some final thoughts on evaluations: Don't overlook using the school's experts (school psychologists and special education teachers) as potential evaluators. Despite my having said that school districts are not looking for more special education candidates, it's been my experience that schools do a very decent job of evaluating children for learning and performance problems, and are actually less apt to diagnose a "disorder" for the reasons mentioned earlier. You should be aware that the opposite is true with private evaluators, who may have a tendency to overdiagnose disorders in order to justify obtaining school services or medication for the child.

> It's been my experience that schools do a very decent job of evaluating children for learning and performance problems.

In any case, the school is obligated by law to perform at least a cursory evaluation called a Student Study Team (or SST) assessment upon the parents' request. If this screening process suggests a more serious learning or behavior problem, schools are then obligated to offer a full IEP evaluation. If a parent is politely persistent, most schools will go through a full evaluation for these children at no cost to the family.

At the opposite extreme, beware of the current fashion of neuropsychological evaluations for potential ADHD. This process often involves hours of testing and may cost up to $6,000. Elaborate and detailed reports running as many as thirty pages are generated. I have yet to read a neuropsychologist's report that didn't find something wrong with a child (a modern-day equivalent of the inkblot Rorschach tests of the Freudian era).

Even when a neuropsychologist has determined a disorder and made recommendations, it's still up to the school to follow through. Without a "buy-in" from the classroom and resource teachers who must implement those recommendations, the

> Without a "buy-in" from the classroom and resource teachers who must implement those recommendations, the [extensive] evaluation does little for the child.

evaluation does little for the child, practically speaking. I've found that, too often, parents are stuck with a long list of recommendations on which no one is likely to follow through.

Which works better for ADHD, isolation or immediate reinforcement?

Here's an apocryphal story to illustrate a point. Mrs. Jones, a third-grade teacher, has been struggling to keep ADHD Johnny focused for the whole year. Finally, the school comes through with a piece of equipment that offers both Johnny and his teacher some hope.

A mobile desk with three walls of soundboard material (as found in office cubicles) is wheeled into the back of the room. When a student moves to the desk, all visual distractions are removed and most sounds are muffled. All the students are eager to try out this new device, which Mrs. Jones describes to the class as "just like your parents' offices."

Mrs. Jones reserves the first opportunity for Johnny. She takes him to the back of the room and, before she pushes his chair into the cubicle, says, "Okay, Johnny, here are ten math problems; I'll be back in ten minutes to check." "Sure, Mrs. Jones," Johnny responds pleasantly.

The lack of an inherent reward for doing the task is a more important factor in attention diverted elsewhere.

Ten minutes later, Mrs. Jones returns to check on Johnny's progress. She finds him playing with his pencil. Johnny sheepishly hands her the worksheet with only two problems completed. "Why haven't you done more, Johnny?" she asks, to which he responds with his usual, "I don't know."

Johnny really wasn't interested in math. If the teacher had removed Johnny's pencil, he would have played with his shirt or even his belly button because either would have been preferable to doing math.

This story illustrates a general misunderstanding about the distractibility and inattentiveness of children with ADHD/ADD. While distracting stimuli play some role in underperformance, the lack of an inherent reward for doing the task is a more important factor in attention diverted elsewhere.

It would be much better for Mrs. Jones to have Johnny sitting right next to her in the front of the class. She should place a timer near him and tell him that if he completes the ten math problems by the time the bell goes off in ten minutes, she will immediately reward him with three M&Ms or with a dollar sign written on a card that he can take home for a reward of money or extra video game time from his parents. If he does a mediocre job, he receives nothing. And if he only completes two or fewer problems, he will have to stay with the teacher for the first five minutes of the next recess.

Here's the moral of this story: To maintain focus, it is much more effective to monitor and immediately reinforce with tangible rewards and punishments than to isolate and remove distracting stimuli. Yet every day, hundreds of thousands of children are isolated at school with no great positive result other than the fact that they are a couple of steps closer to having Ritalin prescribed.

Are there drug alternatives to Ritalin? Or, Strattera: Eli Lilly's great white hope.

During the first part of the twentieth century, an African-American boxer, Jack Johnson, dominated the heavyweight prizefighting world. Racial politics of the day heightened the drama whenever a Caucasian fighter tried to wrest the crown from Johnson—each contender would be coined the next "great white hope."

In the first part of the twenty-first century, Strattera (the brand name for the drug atomoxetine), manufactured and marketed by Eli Lilly, took on Ritalin as the great white hope of ADHD-land. Atomoxetine had been investigated for the treatment of depression in the 1980s, but after Lilly had a huge success with Prozac, they withheld it from the market.

Joseph Biederman and his colleagues at Harvard, who had long been interested in pursuing nonstimulant medications for ADHD, attempted to promote an older antidepressant, desipramine, for ADHD. This attempt ended when several children died suddenly of cardiac arrhythmias while on the drug.

Then, with Lilly's support, they studied atomoxetine and found that it worked better than a placebo, which was all that was needed to obtain FDA approval for release and marketing. Strattera debuted with heretofore unprecedented publicity, hailed as an effective substitute for potentially abusable and addicting stimulant drugs such as Ritalin, Concerta, or Adderall.

I was never impressed with Strattera's PR—plus, my patients generally had success with the stimulant drugs, so I rarely prescribed it. But I only had my guesses to support my decision making. Nearly six years passed before the makers of Concerta conducted a head-to-head trial with Strattera. At equivalent dosages, Strattera was only six-tenths (0.6) as effective against ADHD behavior compared to Concerta. There were also more side effects with Strattera.

Subsequently, both the AAP and AACAP recommend Strattera as a second-choice drug, one that could be tried only if two different stimulants (an amphetamine or methylphenidate-based drug) had first been attempted and had failed. Consequently, Strattera has only a small market share among the myriad of products offered for the treatment of ADHD.

So Eli Lilly is still searching for a drug to replace its blockbuster, Prozac, which became generic early in this decade. Other new nonstimulant drugs, such as Provigil (modafinil) and Intuniv (guanfacine), have been promoted officially and unofficially for ADHD. Like Strattera, they appear to me to be more "great white hopes," unlikely to knock out the still-reigning champ, Ritalin and its variants.

Urban Legend IV: Tourette Syndrome and Ritalin

I had just finished my fellowship in behavioral pediatrics at the University of California, San Francisco, in 1980 when a colleague and friend in the department of neurology, Thomas Lowe, published a paper highlighting a series of children who apparently developed muscle tics while taking Ritalin. Tom's paper struck a chord, and the belief that stimulant drugs could cause tics or hasten the onset of Tourette syndrome (TS) became part of ADHD medication folk wisdom.

I had always wondered about the connection. I had treated hundreds of children with stimulants before ever hearing a report from my patients of tics, which may just have been my good fortune. Subsequently, I have seen several children (including Sam, discussed in Chapter 3) who have had both concurrent ADHD treated with stimulants and tic behavior consistent with TS.

I was not alone in wondering whether Ritalin actually _caused_ the tics.

I was not alone in wondering whether Ritalin actually _caused_ the tics. It turns out that children with TS have much higher rates of ADHD, with or without Ritalin use. Several researchers undertook the laborious task of trying to determine whether Ritalin used for ADHD brought about the tics or made them worse. Kenneth Gadow, a longtime ADHD research psychologist, seemed most determined to settle the Ritalin-tic controversy.

In his definitive study, Gadow had children with TS videotaped when given blinded doses of methylphenidate or a placebo. Based on the severity (frequency and violence) of the tic behavior, neither parents nor children could determine when the real medication was given. Gadow also used blinded researchers to literally count the number of tics within a specified period while the child was both on and off the medication. Again, the researchers could not demonstrate any differences in tic frequency.

Perhaps the best case for using Ritalin for ADHD came from the parents of the children with both ADHD and TS. The vast majority of these parents were clear that they wanted their children to continue to benefit from the stimulant medication despite the possibility that the tics might increase.

Pediatricians were first to relax the prescription of Ritalin in the presence of tics in the mid-1990s (I never stopped prescribing it). It took nearly another ten years for the AACAP to retract their official warning about Ritalin and tic behavior. Still, there are many parents and some doctors who remain sufficiently worried about tics that they avoid the stimulants and use Strattera or Intuniv instead. Neither is nearly as effective as the stimulants, and additionally, they have other potentially more unpleasant or dangerous side effects. It seems that the level of controversy and even paranoia around psychiatric drug use in children is such that once these ADHD-Ritalin myths gain credence, they take a very long time to disappear.

Drug and nondrug interventions for adult ADHD/ADD: Do they work?

Most people would prefer not to take a medication if there were effective nondrug interventions for their daily life problems. Several nondrug approaches have emerged in the treatment of adult ADHD/ADD. They include:

- **Cognitive behavioral training (CBT):** A form of psychotherapy that teaches adults to become more aware of "the basic propositions of living"; for ADHD/ADD, that might include early recognition of falling behind, procrastinating, and behavior that causes others to be frustrated and angry, and then developing and using alternative and more functional approaches.

- **Coaching:** The ADHD/ADD individual hires a person to review his or her habits and goals and develop a plan to address and meet appropriate standards. The process may involve face-to-face meetings, but generally relies primarily on phone calls, email, and texting reminders to follow through and check in.

- **Supportive psychotherapy:** This doesn't necessarily directly address ADHD/ADD but attempts to help the person cope with the fallout of its consequences: anxiety, depression, anger, marital problems, and so on.

- **Career counseling:** The ADHD/ADD individual works with a professional who is familiar with and can guide him or her to a job or profession that best suits the individual's interests, talents, and temperaments; the counselor then takes the individual through the steps necessary to reach that goal.

As of this writing, none of these approaches has demonstrated strong evidence of effectiveness specifically for resolving the problems of adult ADHD/ADD. Russell Barkley and I remain skeptical that cognitive behavioral therapy can make a difference for persons who are impulsive, which is the basic problem and personality issue for those with ADHD. These people already "know" all the rules of behavior but tend to make decisions based on their immediate reactions.

No interventions, drug or nondrug, have been demonstrated to make a long-term difference in quality-of-life markers.

Barkley and I note that ADHD/ADD adults instinctively tend to gravitate to occupations that provide more structure or offer more immediate and intense consequences or pressure: the military, police work, firefighting, and emergency medical response (ambulance or emergency room work). Alternatively, there are occupations or professions for which some degree of eccentricity and/or "hyperfocus" is tolerated or expected, for example, acting, film and theater production, graphic arts, and music performance. The biographies and behaviors of many artists seem consistent with successful ADHD/ADD careers.

Stimulant medications have been shown to improve the symptoms of ADHD/ADD in the short term. But as yet, no interventions, *drug or nondrug*, have been demonstrated to make a long-term difference in quality-of-life markers (including improved economic status and better relationships) for those with adult ADHD/ADD. In their defense, these are difficult, costly studies to perform, and adult ADHD/ADD is still a relatively "new" diagnosis, surfacing initially in the mid- to late 1990s. However, given the history and use of prescription stimulants in adults, I remain skeptical that they will lead to long-term benefits for those who use them.

Urban Legend V:
Brain Scans for ADHD/ADD

We've gone through the "decade of the brain," and these days, brain scans and neuropsychology are in vogue. Clinics have sprung up across the country offering brain scans that will help diagnose specific mental disorders and design specific treatments (primarily drugs) for them. Daniel Amen is one of the most prominent MDs to have

promoted the use of brain scans—
in his case, SPECT, or single photon
emission computed tomography—
as a diagnostic tool. He is the author of many pop psychology books
(among them, *Change Your Brain,
Change Your Life* and *Change Your
Brain, Change Your Body*), and has
even had his own PBS special.

Dr. Amen and his Amen Clinics
are now a national phenomenon,
but I had the good fortune to hear
about and meet Dr. Amen more
than a dozen years ago when his
original clinic was only about thirty
miles from my office. Dr. Amen is a
fabulous and persuasive speaker
and salesman. However, every respected academic neuroradiologist
in the country who has been que-
ried has challenged the science behind his very colorful pictures of his
patients' brains. He recently declined a public request to submit
his scans for review by the Society
of Nuclear Medicine.

In fact, the American Academy
of Child and Adolescent Psychiatry released practice guidelines on
ADHD in 2007, which specifically
declared that brain scans are not
to be used in the evaluation of

Five Proposals for National Reform of the Evaluation and Treatment of ADHD in Children

1. Endeavor to include fathers (including those who are not living in the
home but are still involved with their
children) in all evaluations and treatments of ADHD/ADD.

2. Screen all children referred by
schools for "medical evaluation"
(teacher-speak for ADHD/ADD) at
least minimally for learning and processing weaknesses; these screen-
ings should be handled by the school
psychologist or learning disorders
specialist.

3. Coordinate contacts and interventions of non-school-based professionals involved in the evaluation and
treatment of ADHD/ADD with school
personnel involved with the child.

4. Emphasize and support discipline
strategies that are immediate, tangible, and action-based rather those
that depend on the child's cognition
and conversational interaction.

5. Direct ADHD/ADD counseling approaches toward supporting parents
and teaching them effective behavioral management strategies. Play
therapy specifically meant for the
treatment of ADHD/ADD is not indicated for children.

The American Academy of Child and Adolescent Psychiatry released practice guidelines on ADHD in 2007, which specifically declared that brain scans are not to be used in the evaluation of ADHD at this time.

ADHD at this time. There are simply too many false positives (mistaken cases of a disorder based on a scan) or false negatives (scans that are normal but the person clearly has the disorder) to justify the clinical use of brain scans for ADHD, or for any psychiatric disorder, for that matter. Any children's exposure to radiation involved in these scans is felt to be unnecessary and unwarranted.

Despite this widespread scientific disapproval, Dr. Amen's personal success and the growing use of brain scans for the diagnosis of ADHD attest to the public's desire for clear and quick answers to challenging, problematic, and often messy long-term issues. Brain scans and pop psychology and treatments are yet another caveat emptor (buyer beware) situation for the parents of children with attentional problems.

What books do you recommend for more information on nondrug approaches to ADHD/ADD?

I am regularly asked to recommend books for the treatment of ADHD. If you are interested in a general-information, how-to manual on ADHD and its treatment, consider my second book, *Should I Medicate My Child: Sane Solutions for Troubled Kids With—and Without—Psychiatric Drugs* (Basic, 2002).

However, if you are interested in first pursuing a nondrug approach to your child's problems, I highly recommend two books that are more specific in their approaches than my own. The first is *1-2-3 Magic: Effective Discipline for Children 2–12* by Thomas

Phelan, PhD (ParentMagic Inc., 2009). Dr. Phelan's book is in its fourth edition and has sold more than 1.25 million copies.

His approach ritualizes less talk, fewer chances, and more immediacy of action (time-outs or rewards), which is ideal for many children with or without ADHD. I particularly like his chapters on examples, in which children (from toddler age upward) consciously or unconsciously use a myriad of "techniques" to thwart their parents' resolve. I've used Phelan's book in conjunction with a few of my own suggestions with hundreds of families, and 90 percent of the children have shown at least some immediate improvements.

Phelan feels that his approach is valuable until a child is about twelve. While I would generally agree, I also feel that even for some eleven-year-olds, time-out as a consequence is "lame" and ineffective. At that age (and beyond), a more sophisticated and unfortunately slightly more involved and complex approach to discipline is called for. Fortunately, in his book, *Parenting Your Out-of-Control-Teenager: 7 Steps to Reestablish Authority and Reclaim Love* (St. Martin's Griffin, 2002), Scott Sells provides another relatively straightforward, how-to approach to providing the structure and intensity of rewards and consequences that many, but particularly ADHD, teens and preteens require.

Sells spells out a way for parents to organize their concerns and approaches with their teenager. This process culminates in a "contract" that lays out the specific demands and good and bad consequences for compliance. Parents of teens may smirk and think, "Oh, we've tried contracts before," but I tell you, you haven't seen anything like a Scott Sells contract for rigor and specificity— yet they remain relatively simple (no more than a typewritten page) for the teen and adult to read and sign.

A signature from the teen is not required, however, because the terms go into effect whether or not the teen agrees. Surprisingly, more often than not, the teenager is satisfied with the terms and appreciates the clarity of the rewards. Even more important to the teen, the consequences, which tend to be directed only to weekend activities (no more "You're grounded for a year!"), specifically limit the parents in how much punishment is meted out.

My "success" using *Parenting Your Out-of-Control Teenager* is less than with those ages where I can employ *1-2-3 Magic*. Still, nearly half of the teenagers improve. Moreover, I find that if parents can maintain a modicum of steadiness in their limits and remain available for positive times with their teens, the family can ride out virtually the worst ups and downs the teenage years offer. Parents can at least know they are doing what they can as their youngster matures (finally!).

Ritalin and Growth Delay: Not an Urban Legend

Despite more than seventy years of stimulant use in children with ADHD, debate has continued on whether Ritalin and other similar drugs lead to decreases (temporary or permanent) in children's height. During the 1970s and 1980s, the general and unproven assumption was that stimulants did cause at least a growth delay.

During the 1990s, studies by Joseph Biederman and colleagues at the Massachusetts General Pediatric Psychopharmacology Clinic (which is acknowledged as a strong proponent of psychiatric drug use in children) purported to show that it was the condition of ADHD itself, and not the drugs used to treat it, that was behind some small delays in growth.

However, the government's Multimodal Treatment of Attention Deficit Hyperactivity Disorder (MTA) research published in the late 1990s definitively showed that in the first two years of round-the-clock/year-round (three doses per day, 365 days a year) of Ritalin led to a centimeter (one-half inch) decline in growth compared to children with ADHD who did not take the medication. This decline appeared to last only two years; in subsequent years, the children grew at the same rate as their untreated peers.

Finally, in 2010, definitive comparative studies of children using Ritalin-type drugs long term concluded that there is an ultimate loss of height in these children, about an inch or two on average. For children genetically destined to be of average height, this deficit is likely to be psychologically inconsequential. For children with small parents, this "new" information about the long-term side effects of Ritalin drugs will be weighed against any clear, immediate benefits the medication offers them and their families.

· · ·

An Uneasy Postscript

Are we likely to see a time in the not-so-distant future when a large part of America will be running on Ritalin?

I posed this question in my first book, *Running on Ritalin*, which was written in the mid-1990s. In practice for more than fifteen years at that point, I had already noticed a dramatic change in the types of individuals who were coming to my office for an ADHD diagnosis and a Ritalin prescription. This change and my reactions to it were, in fact, what prompted me to write that book. At the time, ADHD diagnoses and Ritalin use rates were rising steeply, but I had no idea just how profound and widespread an impact this trend would have more than a dozen years in the future.

When I was doing the research for *Running on Ritalin*, I looked for some way to determine how many children were using stimulant medication. There were—and still are—no definitive surveys. However, I knew that the production of Ritalin and other variants of amphetamine prescription stimulants is controlled and regulated by the Drug Enforcement Administration (DEA). Each year, companies that produce controlled substances must apply for approval by the DEA for their annual quota, which the agency routinely grants. The requests and the amounts are recorded in the Federal Register and the DEA also keeps cumulative records.

Upon accessing these records in 1997, I learned that the steep rise in Ritalin production began in 1991, the same year—under heavy pressure from the self-help group CHADD (Children and Adults with Attention Deficit/Hyperactivity Disorder)—the Department of Health and Human Services first included ADHD as a covered diagnosis. This meant that those who had been diagnosed with this condition were entitled to receive special services at school. I also noted that in 1990, the annual quota for methylphenidate (the active ingredient in Ritalin, Concerta, Metadate, and Focalin, among others) was 1,700 kilograms (kg). By 1997, it had risen to 13,824 kilograms, or by more than 700 percent.

I didn't include production quotas for amphetamine (the active ingredient in Adderall and Vyvanse) in *Running on Ritalin* because before 1996, it was less than 1,000 kilograms. Adderall was introduced in the United States in 1996, and the quota for that year was 2,280 kilograms. Now, look at "Annual Production Quotas" on page 237 and check out the production quotas for 2010. For methylphenidate, the DEA approved 50,000,000 kilograms, and for amphetamine, the number is 26,000,000 kilograms. So, for Ritalin-type drugs, the quota had increased by more than 4,000 times, and for the amphetamines, more than 10,000 times.

For Ritalin-type drugs, the quota had increased by more than 4,000 times, and for the amphetamines, more than 10,000 times.

ANNUAL PRODUCTION QUOTAS PER DEA

Amphetamine (Adderall)
1996:   2280 kg
2010:   17,000,000 kg
Up 745,600%

Lisdexamphetamine (Vyvanse)
1996:   0 kg
2010:   9,000,000 kg

Methylphenidate (Ritalin/Concerta)
1996:   11,775 kg
2010:   50,000,000 kg
Up 424,600%

In 2010, American pharmaceutical companies produced 83,776 tons of legal speed for our citizens.

Put into plainer language, in 2010, American pharmaceutical companies produced 83,776 tons of legal speed for our citizens. That translates to more than a half pound of amphetamine-type drugs for every man, woman, and child alive in America today. Assuming that an average dose of Adderall or Vyvanse is 20 milligrams and is taken every day (many children only take medication on school days), 3,562,000 people were using an amphetamine product. Assuming an average 36-milligram dose of Concerta, 3,805,000 were using a methylphenidate product.

I also looked at data provided by the United Nations' International Narcotics Control Board (INCB), based in Vienna, Austria, which maintains records of the amounts of controlled drugs legally produced by each member country. The chart on page 238 shows relative usage rates, based on a number called the divided daily dose (a daily dose, calculated by dividing an approximation of the total amount produced in each country by the number of its citizens). The United States uses twice as much Ritalin-type drugs as Iceland, the

Life must be very tranquil in Brazil, because there, they take only one-hundredth of the legal prescription stimulants that we in America ingest.

second country on the list; three times more than Canada; and ten times more than Germany, Italy, and the United Kingdom. Life must be very tranquil in Brazil, because there, they take only one-hundredth of the legal prescription stimulants that we in America ingest.

U.S. Consumption of Legal Control II Stimulants Compared to Other Countries		
Country	**Total Amount**	**Daily Divided Dose**
United States	18.40	1.00
Iceland	9.20	0.50
Canada	6.71	0.37
Norway	4.33	0.24
Netherlands	3.30	0.18
Israel	3.29	0.18
Australia	2.67	0.15
Germany	2.36	0.13
Denmark	2.25	0.13
Sweden	2.09	0.12
Italy	1.89	0.11
United Kingdom	1.41	0.08
Spain	0.82	0.05
Hong Kong	0.32	0.02
Mexico	0.26	0.02
Japan	0.25	0.02
Brazil	0.17	0.01

Source: 2010 INCB Data

I'm not sure precisely how to interpret this data. I know that much of the rise of legal speed in our country can be attributed to its use by adults, but I have not seen any recent numbers that indicate the percentage prescribed to patients over the age of eighteen. With regard to the international comparisons, America has by far always led in per capita use—one INCB annual report had this subhead: "America loves uppers, Europe loves downers"—which reflects our penchant for stimulants and their preference for minor tranquilizers such as Valium and Xanax.

America loves uppers, Europe loves downers.

Granted, America's influence on international science and culture (strongly supported by the drug industry) has led to an increase in the use of Ritalin-type drugs worldwide, especially in Western Europe, where Scandinavia heads the list. However, we still maintain a healthy lead in their use. What does this say about our country and the ways we choose to cope?

We could speculate that we are pioneers in recognizing that performance problems in general and, more specifically, behavior issues in children are brain-based disorders responsive to drug treatment. Certainly, some of this thinking has influenced other countries. But how can we explain a first-world country like Japan, which consumes only one-fiftieth the amount of Ritalin we do? Clearly, other countries handle issues of both child and adult performance very differently—better or worse, I'm not sure, but definitely differently than we do.

Over the years, I've written three books that in part try to explain what lies behind our national love affair with Ritalin. In *The Last Normal Child*, I proposed that it is our culture's increasing intolerance of minor differences in performance and behavior that has set us on this path. That intolerance is linked to our growing concern about the issue of feelings in general, and particularly our focus—perhaps hyperfocus—on children's self-esteem. We worry so much about how our children feel about themselves that if minor problems are not quickly resolved, we immediately go to doctors for diagnoses and medications. Of course, a huge medical and pharmaceutical industry has developed to foster and profit from that anxiety.

But our worries about our children's feelings don't account for the huge increase in the use of prescription stimulants in adults, the sector that in recent years has shown the greatest growth in sales. America remains the "land of the free"—arguably the least restrictive and unencumbered in terms of material and economic advancement. Continued waves of immigration from both advanced and underdeveloped countries attest to this class mobility. It makes sense, then, that performance enhancers such as Ritalin, Adderall, and Concerta, despite their risks and side effects, are highly attractive to our materialistic meritocracy.

> Performance enhancers such as Ritalin, Adderall, and Concerta, despite their risks and side effects, are highly attractive to our materialistic meritocracy.

My son Martin and I recently had an intense conversation about the illegal use of Adderall by college students. As Martin, who is twenty-three and entering a graduate program in music, told me, "Dad, over fifty percent of my friends have used Adderall illegally. It's really weird. They don't think there's anything wrong about using it to study, stay up, or even get high. You have to get the word out. Not enough people know about this. And what does it say about our values?"

He raises an excellent point. Earlier in this book, I suggested that college students ask themselves a series of questions if they felt they needed to regularly employ a prescription stimulant to cope with school or life. But I don't think this sort of self-reflective questioning will do much to alter most people's use of Ritalin-type drugs, either legitimately or illegally. Societal influences and pressures are too great. It makes me sad to think that young and otherwise normal adults feel their performance is so threatened that they are drawn to using Ritalin to cope. I think especially of Katie's feelings about herself, and her dilemma over restarting Adderall. I totally understand these pressures, and do not condemn Katie or other students for their decision to use a drug to help themselves for the short or even the long term. But like my son, I wonder about the strengths and weaknesses of our society; every culture has both. As far as I can tell, there are no powerful or effective countertrends on the horizon that will offset our quest for material satisfaction as a way to achieve spiritual and emotional contentment.

> There are no powerful or effective countertrends on the horizon that will offset our quest for material satisfaction as a way to achieve spiritual and emotional contentment.

As helpful as these drugs can be to children and adults, they carry a risk—primarily to adults—of abuse and addiction. The risk may be small (perhaps less than one in ten) but it is significant. We are beginning to see the casualties: increasing emergency room visits to treat overdoses of prescription stimulants; hospital and rehabilitation admissions for abusive and addictive behavior; and most critically, countless lives ruined by those who began with a prescription stimulant and moved on to cocaine and methamphetamine abuse.

Earlier in this book, I mentioned a period during which women were routinely prescribed prescription stimulants (amphetamines) for weight reduction and control. Eventually, it became clear that these stimulants' long-term benefits were nil and the risks of addiction were high. Even then, it took a unique coalition—which included an aggressive FDA commissioner and newly empowered feminists, who rejected patriarchal pharmacologically derived body images—to force local and state medical licensing boards to take action against doctors who continued to prescribe amphetamines. Politicians and the media joined the antidrug forces, and by the late 1970s, the use of amphetamines for weight control had markedly diminished. At the time of this writing in 2010, I can neither see nor predict such a coalition forming to speak out against the overuse of Ritalin for ADHD-type behavior or general performance enhancement.

I dwell in a contradiction, however. In my writings, I've examined my role as a physician who prescribes these drugs. I've explained my ambivalences and ethical quandaries. My job as a physician is to relieve suffering, and I believe that, despite claims by antipsychiatry critics, children and adults are genuinely suffering as a result of performance and behavioral difficulties. So I will prescribe Ritalin even when I feel these difficulties are relatively minor. But to avoid being complicit in the problem, I must raise questions and consciousness about the societal forces that have potential for unintentional negative consequences. The practice of using performance-enhancing drugs for the treatment of a disorder or improving a lifestyle may make sense for the individual. But I deeply worry about an America running on Ritalin, because a society that copes with life's challenges by using a drug does so at its own peril.

ENDNOTES

16   *[Special ed] has never proven that it can change the basic abilities of children.* Detterman, DK, and Thompson, LA. What is so special about special education? *Am Psychologist* 52: 1082–90, 1997.

18   *Today, at least one in ten eleven-year-old boys take Ritalin equivalents.* Castle, L, Aubert, RE, Verbrugge, RR, et al. Trend in medication treatment for ADHD. *J Atten Disorders* 10: 335–42, 2007.

18   *Some college campuses report that more than one-third of their students.* Low, KG, and Gendaszek, AE. Illicit use of psychostimulants among college students: a preliminary study. *Psycho Health Med* 7: 283–87, 2002.

18   *That has been compared to a steroid for the brain.* Greely, H, Sahakian, B, Harris, J, et al. Towards responsible use of cognitive-enhancing drugs by the healthy. *Nature* 456: 702–5, 2008.

33   *He coauthored with Kevin R. Murphy and Mariellen Fischer.* Barkley, RA, Murphy, KR, and Fischer, M. *ADHD in Adults: What the Science Says.* New York: Guilford Press, 2008.

36   *A summary of Barkley's research on ADHD children in adulthood.* Antshel, KM, and Barkley, R. Developmental and behavioral disorders grown up: attention deficit hyperactivity disorder. *J Dev Behav Pediatr* 30: 81–90, 2009.

42   *Minimum of twenty years to get "unbiased" results.* Jensen, PS. ADHD in Adults: What the Science Says (book review). *J Atten Disorders* 13: 97–98, 2009.

46   *On one hand, we have* The Gift of ADHD. Honos-Webb, L. *The Gift of ADHD: How to Transform Your Child's Problems into Strengths.* Oakland, Calif.: New Harbinger Publications, 2005.

104   *"Early Adolescence," in* The Last Normal Child. Diller, LH. *The Last Normal Child: Essay on the Intersection of Kids, Culture and Psychiatric Drugs.* Westport, Conn.: Praeger Publishers, 2006, pp. 78–86.

116   *As described in the popular parenting guide* 1-2-3 Magic. Phelan, T. *1-2-3 Magic: Effective Discipline for Children 2–12, Third Edition.* Glen Ellyn, Ill.: ParentMagic Inc., 2003.

126   *Problems of school-age children with ADHD.* Mrug, S, Hoza, B, Pelham, WE, et al. Behavior and peer status in children with ADHD: Continuity and change. *J Atten Disorders,* 10: 359–71, 2007. Hinshaw, SP, and Melnick, SM. Peer relationships in boys with attention-deficit hyperactivity disorder with and without comorbid aggression. *Dev & Psychopathology,* 63: 41–50, 1995.

145   *A study of children diagnosed with both ADHD and ODD.* Satterfield, JH, Faller, KJ, Crinella, FM, et al. A 30-year prospective follow-up study of hyperactive boys with conduct problems: adult criminality. *J Am Acad Child Adolesc Psychiatry,* 46: 601–10, 2007.

167   *To ADHD children who weren't given the medication.* Lambert, NM, and Hartsough, CS. Prospective study of tobacco smoking and substance dependencies among samples of ADHD and non-ADHD participants. *J Learning Disorders,* 31: 533–44, 1998.

168   *Used Ritalin were abusing less as adults.* Biederman, J, Wilens, T, Mick, E, et al. Pharmacotherapy of attention-deficit/hyperactivity disorder reduces risk for substance use disorder. *Pediatrics* 104: e20, 1999.

169   *Nor protected them from future drug abuse.* Barkley, RA, Fischer, M, Smallish, L, et al. Does the treatment of attention-deficit/hyperactivity disorder with stimulants contribute to drug/use abuse? A 13-year prospective study. *Pediatrics* 111: 1–13, 2003.

169   *Has been documented since their synthesis in 1929.* Rasmussen, N. *On Speed: The Many Lives of Amphetamine.* New York: New York University Press, 2008.

170   *Has admitted to the illegal use of a prescription stimulant.* Low, KG, and
      Gendaszek, AE. Illicit use of psychostimulants among college students.

170   *Among the fraternity-sorority subpopulation at the school.* 60 Minutes,
      "Boosting Brain Power," April 25, 2010. www.cbsnews.com/video/watch/
      ?id=6430949n.

171   *Prestigious journals such as* Nature. Greely, H, et al. Towards responsible
      use of cognitive-enhancing drugs.

171   *Consistent with abuse and addiction.* Kroutil, LA, Van Brunt, DL, Herman-
      Stahl, MA, et al. Nonmedical use of prescription stimulants in the United
      States. *Drug and Alcohol Dependence,* 84: 135–43, 2006.

193   *Children are a product of genes and biology.* Harris, J. *The Nurture Assump-
      tion: Why Children Turn Out the Way They Do.* New York: Free Press, 1998.

200   *My first major article on ADHD and Ritalin.* Diller, LH. The run on Ritalin:
      attention deficit disorder and stimulant medication treatment in the 1990s.
      Hastings Center Report 26: 12–18, 1996.

200   *A request by the* New York Times. Kolata, G. Boom in Ritalin sales raises
      ethical questions. *New York Times,* May 15, 1996, p. C8.

207   *Its potential for increasing suicidal thinking.* Leslie, LK, Newman, TB,
      Chesney, JC, et al. The Food and Drug Administration's deliberations on
      antidepressant use in pediatric patients. *Pediatrics* 116: 195–204, 2005.

208   *Amphetamine on children's hyperactive behavior.* Bradley, C. The behavior
      of children receiving Benzedrine. *Am J Psychiatry* 94: 577–85, 1937.

209   *Same on children with and without ADHD.* Rapoport, JL, Buchsbaum, MS,
      et al. Dextroamphetamine: Its cognitive and behavioral effects in normal
      and hyperactive boys and normal men. *Arch Gen Psychiatry* 37: 933–43,
      1980.

211   *A noted ADHD researcher; it was published in 1994.* Hoover, DW, and
      Milich, R. Effects of sugar ingestion expectancies on mother-child interac-
      tions. *J Abnormal Child Psychology* 22: 510–15, 1994.

212   *Make children more irritable and restless.* Rowe, KS, and Rowe, KJ. Syn-
      thetic food coloring and behavior: a dose response effect in a double-
      blind, placebo controlled, repeated-measure study. *J Pediatrics* 125: 691–98,
      1994.

213   *Up to six capsules are required daily.* Sinn, N, and Bryan, J. Effect of supplementation with polyunsaturated fatty acids and micronutrients on learning and behavior problems associated with child ADHD. *J Dev Behav Pediatrics* 28: 82–91, 2007.

213   *Nothing definitive has been published.* Busch, B. Polyunsaturated fatty acid supplementation for ADHD? Fishy, fascinating, and far from clear. *J Dev Behav Pediatrics* 28: 139–44, 2007.

214   *Decreases the need for a medication intervention.* Boyce, WT, Essex, MJ, Alkon, A, et al. Early father involvement moderates biobehavioral susceptibility to mental health problems in middle childhood. *J Am Acad Child Adolesc Psychiatry* 45: 1510–20, 2006.

224   *Conducted a head-to-head trial with Strattera.* Newcorn, JH, Kratochvil, CJ, Allen, AJ, et al. Atomoxetine and osmotically released methylphenidate for the treatment of attention deficit hyperactivity disorder: acute comparison and differential response. *Am J Psychiatry* 165: 721–30, 2008.

225   *Developed muscle tics while taking Ritalin.* Lowe, TL, Cohen, DJ, Kremenitzer, MW, et al. Stimulant medications precipitate Tourette's syndrome. *JAMA* 247: 1729–31, 1982.

226   *Blinded doses of methylphenidate or a placebo.* Gadow, KD, Sverd, J, Nolan, EE, et al. Immediate-release methylphenidate for ADHD in children with comorbid chronic multiple tic disorder. *J Am Acad Child Adolesc Psychiatry* 46: 840–48, 2007.

229   *Author of many pop psychology books.* Amen, DG. *Change Your Brain, Change Your Life.* New York: Three Rivers Press, 2000. Amen, DG. *Change Your Brain, Change Your Body.* New York: Harmony Books, 2010.

229   *For review by the Society of Nuclear Medicine.* Adinoff, B, and Devous, M. Scientifically unfounded claims in diagnosing and treating patients (letter). *Am J Psychiatry* 167: 598, 2010.

229   *Not to be used in the evaluation of ADHD at this time.* AACAP Official Action. Practice parameter for the assessment and treatment of children and adolescents with attention-deficit/hyperactivity disorder. *J Am Acad Child Adolesc Psychiatry* 46: 894–921, 2007.

230 *The growing use of brain scans for the diagnosis of ADHD.* AACAP Official Action. Practice parameter for the assessment and treatment of children and adolescents with attention-deficit/hyperactivity disorder. *J Am Acad Child Adolesc Psychiatry* 46: 894–921, 2007.

232 *Behind some small delays in growth.* Spencer, TJ, Biederman, J, Harding, M, et al. Growth deficits in ADHD children revisited: evidence for disorder-associated growth delays? *J Am Acad Child Adolesc Psychiatry* 35: 1460–69, 1996.

233 *With ADHD who did not take the medication.* Vitello, B, Severe, JB, Greenhill, L, et al. Methylphenidate dosage for children with ADHD over time under controlled conditions: lessons from the MTA. *J Am Acad Child Adolesc Psychiatry* 40: 188–96, 2001.

233 *An inch or two on average.* Poulton, A. Growth on stimulant medication; clarifying the confusion: a review. *Arch Dis Child* 90: 801–6, 2005.

236 *Check out the production quotas for 2010.* Drug Enforcement Administration. www.deadiversion.usdoj.gov/quotas/quota_history.pdf.

237 *Legally produced by each member country.* International Narcotics Control Board. Psychotropic substances-technical report (report 2009; statistics for 2008), Table IV.1 (page 267). www.incb.org/incb/psychotropics_reports .html.

INDEX